SOCIAL CASE WORK:
GENERIC AND SPECIFIC

A REPORT OF THE
MILFORD CONFERENCE

SOCIAL CASE WORK

Generic and Specific

❦ ❦

An Outline

A Report of the Milford Conference

Studies in the Practice of Social Work No. 2

Published by

AMERICAN ASSOCIATION OF SOCIAL WORKERS
NEW YORK

————————

CLASSIC SERIES
NATIONAL ASSOCIATION OF SOCIAL WORKERS

National Association of Social Workers
1425 H Street NW
Washington, D.C. 20005

_____

First Printing, June, 1929.
Second Printing, January, 1931.
Third Printing, May, 1935.

Reprinted 1974
Copyright © 1974 by the National Association of
Social Workers, Inc.
International Standard Book No. 0-87101-069-0
Library of Congress Catalog Card No. 74-83097
NASW Publication No. CBC-069-C
Printed in the USA 1974

FOREWORD TO THE 1974 EDITION

By and large, social workers have taken a less-than-enthusiastic interest in the history of our profession. This may reflect nothing more than the general preference of the society at large for the present and the future over the past, but it is unfortunate nonetheless. As social work historians have repeatedly shown, better understanding of professional origins can illuminate present problems in useful ways. A timely example is *Social Case Work: Generic and Specific — A Report of the Milford Conference,* here republished by the successor to the professional organization that originally issued it in 1929.

The concerns that gave rise to the Milford Conference report bear a striking similarity to those that trouble many social workers today. In the 1920s the profession was starting to divide itself into a growing array of specialties. Practitioners in each specialty, typically identified with specific kinds of agencies, formed their own organizations that tended to emphasize the differences separating them from other social workers. The question inevitably arose: *Are there sufficient commonalities among the various specialties to preserve the idea that all social workers are part of one profession?*

This question was a central concern of the Milford Conference, and the answer given in the report greatly influenced the subsequent course of the profession. The report concluded, unequivocally, that the similarities among the various specialties overshadowed their differences and practitioners in the specialties required a common knowledge base and, therefore, common training programs. Thus the concept of generic social work was born, or at least took form and substance in this report.

Although the report is remembered for its support of generic social work, it placed equal emphasis on other recommendations that, unfortunately, have had less influence on the profession. For example, there are two recommendations throughout the report which, if they had been heeded, would have helped the profession with some of the problems it now faces. One was that while the principles and concepts developed by the profession and described in the report are promising and useful, they are vague and in need of more precise specification. The second was an urgent call for increased research activity in the profession, especially for the creation of a cadre of practitioner-researchers who understand both practice and research.

It is hoped that this reissue by the Publications Committee of the National Association of Social Workers will stimulate thought and discussion about the issues addressed in the report — issues that will persist for some time. The report does not and cannot solve our current and future problems, but it provides a necessary background for understanding them.

SCOTT BRIAR — Member
Publications Committee
National Association of Social Workers

May 1974
Seattle, Washington

FOREWORD

The American Association of Social Workers welcomes the opportunity to publish the *Milford Conference Report*, as the second volume in "Studies in the Practice of Social Work." The expressed purpose of this series is to preserve and distribute the results of studies and research going on in the field. The first volume in the series is, *Interviews, A Study of the Methods of Analyzing and Recording Case Work Interviews*, by a Committee of the Chicago Chapter of the Association. A third volume, *Social Work Ethics*, by Lula Jean Elliott, has been published since the first printing of the *Milford Conference Report*.

The origin and make up of the Milford Conference are explained in the report. The report itself deals with difficult problems which have followed the tendency to develop specialized forms of social case work under different agency auspices. Social workers are aware of these problems, but this report makes an important contribution by its manner of sorting the problems into an orderly outline, thus laying bare the relationships of the problems to each other, and by indicating the parts of the pattern that need to be filled in by further study and research.

The method of the study is also important to social workers. One of the handicaps to the development of a social work literature has been the constant application required of the practitioner to his job, and the scant provision available for the deliberation and study needed for critical discussion. The early chapters of the volume reveal the process by which a committee meeting only at intervals developed from a group of persons with individualized interests and with limited amount of time into a compact, productive unit.

Publication by the Association does not endorse the conclusions reached by the Milford Conference. The report and its point of view and conclusions is presented with full confidence that the document will be stimulating to a wide range of social workers and to others interested in the problems of organization, interpretation and training.

WALTER WEST, Executive Secretary
American Association of Social Workers

TABLE OF CONTENTS

PART I

INTRODUCTION AND SUMMARY

CHAPTER I
REASONS FOR THIS STUDY

In October, 1923, seventeen executives and board members from six national organizations in the social case work field met for a two-day conference at Milford, Pennsylvania. Thus began the so-called Milford Conference which found its first meeting so valuable that it has continued to hold a two-day annual conference ever since. The spirit and method of even earlier informal gatherings, beginning perhaps in February, 1921, have carried over—even as the objectives have become a little clearer. Believing that "minds work by contagion and sciences grow by communication" the Milford Conference sought to place the sharing of viewpoints ahead of the formulation of knowledge. The processes of professional companionship and silent encouragement seemed more important than the information any one person might have to impart. The absence of an organized program yielded quick recognition of common problems, one of which has come to claim careful and sustained study.

At the first meeting of the Milford Conference an attempt was made to define the several fields of social case work. The discussion made it clear that the group were not able at that time to define social case work itself so as to distinguish it sharply from other forms of professional work nor the separate fields of social case work so as to differentiate them sharply from each other. At the same session of the Conference there was a discussion of training for social case work which did not lead to any fruitful formulations of training programs.

At subsequent sessions of the Conference the same two subjects were dealt with and each was made the special subject of consideration by subcommittees appointed to prepare reports during the interim between meetings of the Conference as a whole. While these discussions led to no formulations of practical value, they served to clarify some of the problems facing social case workers. Their most important result, perhaps, was the emergence of a strong conviction unanimously held by the members of the Conference that a fundamental conception which had come to be spoken of as "generic social case work" was much more substantial in content and much more significant in its implications for all forms of social case work than were any of the specific emphases of the different case work fields. This conception was in no sense original with the Milford Conference, but it seemed doubtful whether the conception had previously been so continuously discussed and deliberately accepted by so large a group of social case workers.

The emergence of this degree of unanimity regarding the paramount importance of generic social work was something more than an academic result of the Conference discussions. It reflected the whole point of view of modern social case work as it is practiced in the field. It seemed to the members of the Conference, that the implications of this conception should be explored. Here, however, the Conference encountered difficulties. Its membership included about twenty-five persons who had or were having authoritative experience in the field of social case work. There was no doubt but that in practice social case workers had become increasingly sure-footed in their use of the concepts, facts and methods which constitute social case work, but it was equally apparent that practice had developed more rapidly than the contemplation of its significance, or the ability to define it.

A second result of these discussions was a recognition of the importance of the problems of division of labor among case work agencies. This, again, was not a new question. It has furnished material for discussion for a generation. After a generation's discussion, however, it seemed to the group that dividing lines between the specific fields of social case work were still lacking, as well as the fundamental principles underlying the practical working divisions among the case work agencies of a community. Here, again, it was apparent that, despite the difficulties which the problem of the division of labor was creating in many places, the practice of social case work revealed ample evidence that here and there progress had been made toward a solution of the problem. It had usually been solved on a highly opportunist basis. The Conference was unable to decide with any conviction that there was a philosophy governing the division of labor or any broad principles of universal application to guide the agencies of a community in working out their relationships to each other. Here was another phase of social case work in which practice had outrun formulation.

A third result of these discussions was the conviction that, while the trained worker was a fact, nobody knew how he came to be a fact. The differences between a trained worker and an untrained one were sufficiently apparent but the content of a training program was still to be formulated. This does not mean that social case work had made no deliberate efforts at training. On the contrary, deliberate training programs were over a quarter of a century old when the Milford Conference first came into session. Substantial apprentice programs came into existence in the last decade of the nineteenth century and the first training school was established two years before the nineteenth century closed. Somehow or other social case workers were learning and were being assisted to learn how to do social case work. Nevertheless, when the Conference attempted to define the content of training programs in terms of the requirements of the specific fields of social case work, it discovered once more that practice had outrun thinking.

After these and other matters pertaining to social case work had been discussed at four successive meetings of the Milford Conference, a special committee was appointed in the hope that its members could, by concentrating upon the specific questions which embody the subject matter of this report, produce some formulations regarding the meaning of social case work and its practice.

At the Milford Conference held October 23, 1925, the Chairman was authorized to appoint a committee of five without reference to representation of fields but to represent solely the Milford Conference as a whole, which should prepare for the Conference a report covering the following points:

1. What can we understand by generic social case work?
2. Assuming competent agencies in the various case work fields, what is a desirable basis for a division of labor in social case work in a local community?
3. What is a competent agency for social case work?
4. What constitutes training for social work?

The Committee appointed to carry out this assignment consisted of Harriet E. Anderson, C. C. Carstens, Mary C. Hurlbutt, Margaret E. Rich, and Porter R. Lee, Chairman. At the end of the first year, Miss Hurlbutt resigned from the Committee when she took up her new duties with the International Migration Service in Geneva and M. Antoinette Cannon was appointed to succeed her. Christine Robb participated in one meeting of the Committee as representative of psychiatric social work.

This volume embodies the final report of the Committee as accepted by the Milford Conference at its meeting November 9-10, 1928.

Following is a list of members of the Milford Conference. Not all the members have been present at each meeting: Harriet E. Anderson, C. W. Areson, Mrs. Marjorie Bell, Rhea Kay Boardman, Mary Bogue, M. Antoinette Cannon, Ida Cannon, C. C. Carstens, Florence Cassidy, C. L. Chute, Jane F. Culbert, Ida Curry, Edith Everett, Julia George, Mrs. John M. Glenn, David H. Holbrook, Mary Hurlbutt, Cheney Jones, Dorothy C. Kahn, Virginia Kelly, Anna Kempshall, Mrs. Kathleen Ormsby Larkin, Ruth Larned, Porter R. Lee, Francis H. McLean, Margaret Steel Moss, Emma Phinney, Anna B. Pratt, Georgia Ralph, Margaret E. Rich, Christine C. Robb, Mildred Scoville, Mrs. Maida H. Solomon, Linton B. Swift, Frances Taussig, Janet Thornton, Henry W. Thurston, Ruth Taylor, Lena R. Waters.

The members have been definitely interested in some one of the fields of social case work represented by the following organizations: Family Welfare Association of America, American Association of Hospital Social Workers, American Association of Psychiatric Social Workers, Child Welfare League of America, International Migration Service, National Association of Travelers' Aid Societies, National Committee on Visiting Teachers, National Probation Association.

CHAPTER II

Procedure of the Conference and the Committee

The members of the Milford Conference and other social case workers have doubtless been in a mood to welcome any statements in regard to social case work which would clear up some of the confusion, uncertainty and lack of precision which characterizes much of our thinking about social case work and our practice to no small extent. We may have hoped that a Committee working for three years on this assignment could produce a document which would at once establish social case work as definite, precise and scientific. This report may seem like a meager result of three years' work. It does little more than to define the problem which was in the minds of the Conference when the Committee was appointed and to suggest certain directions in which social case workers might proceed with the expectation of contributing to its solution.

The Conference believes that the report submitted is the best of which it was capable under the circumstances. The circumstances have been the limitation of time available for Committee work in the programs of five busy persons and the absence of any considerable amount of assembled data concerning social case work. It believes that the report as submitted gains in significance if considered in connection with the procedure followed by the Committee in its preparation. The work of the Committee can be divided into three stages: the first year, 1925-26, during which practically no progress was made; the second year, 1926-27, at the end of which time a report covering the first of the four questions assigned was presented to the Conference; and the third year, 1927-28, during which the Committee covered the other three questions in its assignment and presented its final report to the Conference.

During the first year, following the conventional practice of committees under such circumstances, we held several meetings varying in length from one and one-half hours to seven hours each, devoting our time to attempts to find our way into the assignment. The five members of the Committee approached the task convinced that there is such a thing as generic social case work. Our discussions during the first year, however, were colored by the fact that we had each of us been more or less immersed in the problems of specific fields and that we had, also, individually attempted at various times some analysis of generic social case work which had, to a large extent, crystallized our thinking. The difficulty of breaking through these mental crystallizations was, we believe, not wholly temperamental but was inherent in the conditions under which committees made up of busy persons ordinarily attempt to carry out such assignments as this.

It seemed logical to begin our work with an attempt to answer the first question, "What is generic social case work?" It seemed logical, also, to prepare for the Committee's discussions of this question by asking each member to work out an outline of generic social case work. The result was five outlines, upon each of which one member of the Committee had spent a considerable amount of time and into which he had put many of the conclusions arrived at in a professional life-time and with which he was naturally more satisfied than he was likely to be with a different outline. The result was that our discussions usually began with an attempt to reconcile differences instead of attempting to find something new. The psychological difficulties of accomplishing anything on this basis in relatively brief meetings held at long intervals are obvious. At the end of the first year, we had arrived nowhere and so reported to the Conference. The one hopeful thing about the Committee's studies at this time was its decision to begin a second year's work with a three-day conference held away from New York.

This three-day conference began the second stage of the Committee's program in the second year of its activity. At this conference the Committee abandoned all preconceived notions of social case work and of the differences and likenesses of the various specific fields and set itself the task of listing the items which make up the subject matter of social case work. No attempt was made to classify them or to evaluate them in the first instance but merely to secure a comprehensive list. As the items were suggested in turn by members of the Committee, they were recorded on a master list. No disagreement was permitted; the desire of any member of the group to have an item on the list insured its being placed there. The process of building up the list continued until no member of the Committee could think of anything to add. The list was made more comprehensive later after a review by members of the Committee of a substantial amount of the literature on social case work, including the Proceedings of the National Conference, volumes of "The Family" and many of the outstanding books relating to the subject. By these two bits of procedure a list of approximately five hundred items was made. After considerable discussion the classifications which furnish the headings of the first seven chapters of Part II of this report were adopted. None of the approximately five hundred items which the Committee finally recorded as significant failed to classify under one of these headings. The Committee, therefore, decided that the whole nature and scope of social case work could be adequately discussed under these headings, although it recognizes the possibility of many other valid classifications.

The next step was to scrutinize the original list in order to rule out duplications and irrelevancies. Some further deletions were made in the interest of a simplified list and further modifications were suggested at the meeting of the Milford Conference in the fall of 1927. The remaining items were embodied in a separate list given at the beginnings of the first seven chapters of Part II of this report.

The final step in the preparation of its answer to the first question in its assignment was to discuss the implications of these lists of items. It was at this stage that the unevenness of the development of social case work as a science and a profession became most clearly apparent. It was relatively easy, for example, to make up a list of what the Committee has termed "deviations from accepted standards of normal life," (Part II, Chapter V) because these deviations are clearly recognized in social case work and practice is influenced by the social case worker's conception of their significance. The Committee found, however, that social case workers are very much more precise in their understanding of some of these deviations than they are of others. "Delinquency" and "dependent widowhood" for example, are familiar conceptions. Social case workers cannot pretend to know all of their implications and yet they are much more sure-footed in their understanding of them than they are of "instability" or of "foreignness," to take two other terms which appear on this list.

Furthermore, the Committee discovered that with respect to some of the major divisions of the lists—methods, for example, there is a greater accumulation of established fact and tested experience than is true of some other divisions, such as the adaptation of science and experience.

To a considerable extent, therefore, the discussions of the Committee thus far pointed towards two objectives: first, to indicate the significance for social case work of each of the groups of items presented in Chapters V-XI in Part II, and second, to suggest places at which there seemed to be the greatest need for research and study in order to clarify thinking and stabilize practice. The results of these discussions by the Committee, together with the lists of items, make up the contents of Chapters V-XI of Part II and represent, also, the fruit of the second stage of the Committee's procedure.

The third stage of the Committee's work began after the meeting of the Milford Conference in October, 1927. At this Conference the preliminary report, embodying the suggestions of the Committee for an answer to question I, had been submitted and certain revisions were proposed by the Conference. The Conference voted to continue the Committee and to refer back to it this preliminary report with suggested revisions and to leave the Committee free to determine its own procedure from that point.

Two courses seemed open. The Committee might embody the revisions suggested by the Conference in a preliminary report and proceed to the preparation of answers to the other three questions in its original assignment or it might defer work on the other questions and undertake more intensive study of one of the many phases of social case work which its preliminary report indicated to be badly in need of exploration and research. The Committee decided upon the first alternative.

Report of the Milford Conference

The second year's work had developed so stable a basis of common understanding among the members of the Committee that they were able to undertake the final stage with less risk of wasting time in the reconciliation of unnecessarily divergent points of view. Answers to the remaining three questions proved hardly less elusive than had been an answer to the first one. In the end, the answers arrived at by the Committee were similar to its suggestions regarding the first question. That is to say, they are presented in the form of outlines of what answers might be with as much discussion of detail as seemed safely within the bounds of established practice, and, therefore, not too much within the area of sheer speculation and opinion.

The Committee, during the third stage, has for the most part followed the plan developed in the second year of meeting never less than a full day at a time and usually for two or three days. This plan has enabled them to conserve momentum and has contributed to concentration and unhurried thinking and developed a kind of solidarity of understanding on the part of the Committee, which in its judgment has made its production in this report more substantial than its members could have been capable of under any other circumstances.

In addition to twenty meetings (totaling thirty days) of the Committee, each member of the Committee has devoted a considerable amount of time between meetings to the preparation of material and interviews with persons outside the Committee membership from whom it seemed desirable to secure data of one kind or another. The Committee has made considerable use of persons outside its membership in connection with the formulations of specific subject matter which constitute an especially important part of the content of Part III.

CHAPTER III
THE NATURE OF THIS REPORT

After three years of work this Committee presents its report in the form of a comprehensive outline of social case work, its organization and its practice. It became apparent to the Committee early in its deliberations that adequate answers to the four questions constituting its assignment could not be made within the time available for Committee work. Furthermore, the Committee believes that many of the implications of these questions cannot be satisfactorily discussed without the assembling through research of data which are not now available. In these circumstances it seemed that the most helpful service the Committee could render would be to prepare an outline of the subject matter assigned to it, including as much detail as the Committee was able to record with some confidence of its soundness, and presenting the whole report in such a way as to indicate where research and study of social work by social case workers is needed. In a sense the Committee is presenting a bare structure in the hope that it may stimulate, guide and give coherence to the efforts of social workers throughout the country to study their own professional problems and equipment.

The material has been organized under four headings, corresponding to the four questions assigned by the Conference. The Committee has attempted to analyze the subject matter of each of these four questions into several main sub-divisions. The discussion under these main sub-divisions, all of which are indicated in the Table of Contents, varies in character. In some instances the Committee has been able to do no more than to indicate in the sketchiest fashion what seems to it the significance of these sub-divisions. In other cases it has tried to formulate what seem to it legitimate conclusions. For the most part, however, the discussions under the various main divisions of the report are general in character and designed to be suggestive of fruitful leads to research, to working principles, to significant aspects of current practice in social case work or to aspects of social case work which have already been authoritatively discussed elsewhere.

While the Committee believes that the most important formulations regarding the problems and equipment of social case work are still to be made, it also believes that the sub-divisions presented in this report under the four major questions assigned it represent an illuminating and comprehensive classification. That the detailed discussions of the report are not more substantial is partly due to the limitations of time, partly to the limitations in the Committee itself and partly to the present nebulous state of much of the subject matter of social case work. The Committee would like to point out further that it believes that there is nothing in the report which does not reflect actual practice somewhere in the field. Social case work throughout the country is uneven in its standards and in its results. The full implications of the report are probably realized by no one agency and in no one field. Nevertheless, the Committee believes that every suggestion made has been tested and found practicable somewhere in the practice of social case work agencies in the United States.

The Committee's Conclusions in Regard to Its Assignment

The Committee's conclusions after three years of work on this assignment are embodied in the report itself. It wishes, however, to emphasize the following:

1. Social case work is a definite entity. It has a field increasingly well defined, it has all of the aspects of the beginnings of a science in its practice and it has conscious professional standards for its practitioners. The various separate designations (children's case worker, family case worker, probation officer, visiting teacher, psychiatric social worker, medical social worker, etc.) by which its practitioners are known tend to have no more than a descriptive significance in terms of the type of problem with which they respectively deal. They have relatively less significance all the time in terms of the professional equipment which they connote in comparison with the generic term "social case work." This report testifies to the importance of the specific fields of social case work and to the specific demands which each specific field makes upon case workers practicing within it. Nevertheless, the outstanding fact is that the problems of social case work and the equipment of the social case worker are fundamentally the same for all fields. In other words, in any discussion of problems, concepts, scientific knowledge or methods, generic social case work is the common field to which the specific forms of social case work are merely incidental.

2. At the present time the practice of social case work is more precise than the formulations of philosophy, knowledge, methods and experience. As we have said before this is not a new discovery. It is, however, a fact which has been borne in upon the Committee with renewed significance. That this should be so is undoubtedly evidence of a healthier state than would be the case if formulations had the appearance of greater precision than practice. Nevertheless, this situation must be remedied if social case work is to develop.

3. The remedy for the situation in the judgment of the Committee is clear. Social case workers must become more energetic in pursuing penetrating study and research in their professional subject matter. We believe that this report outlines a content for social case work sufficiently substantiated in its implications to justify the claim that social case work is potentially both scientific in character and professonal in its practice. Scientific and pro-

fessional, however, are terms which can at the present time justifiably be applied to social case work chiefly because of its potentialities.

There are, nevertheless, as this report indicates, many aspects of social case work which are so well established as to justify thinking of them as both scientific and professional in their significance. This report has assembled from the terminology of social case work a variety of terms in current use, each of which has a meaning for those who use it. The meanings, however, vary greatly in definiteness. For illustration, take the five terms "interviewing," "social service exchange," "participation," "personality" and "the psychology of failure." Each one of them has for the social case worker a technical significance. Each one connotes something in the equipment of social case work which is being used with constantly increasing effectiveness. If the Committee were to attempt, however, to define these terms as used by the social case worker, it would find it difficult to make the definitions equally precise. This is partly because social case workers and others know less about some of them than about others. It is, however, true that the use of some of these terms would suggest a greater knowledge of their implications than the Committee's discussion of them would indicate.

The conclusion of the Committee on this point is that there is no greater responsibility facing social case work at the present time than the responsibility of organizing continuous research into the concepts, problems and methods of its field. There is need not for one treatise on social case work but for a library of treatises. Social case workers cannot leave the responsibility for research to foundations and universities. They must do it themselves and participation by social case workers in such research must be widespread. The results of such studies embodied in articles, papers, pamphlets, monographs and books are needed for the training of case workers. They are needed for the development of sounder methods of supervision in social case work agencies and they are needed for the service of the individual social case worker in his own professional development.

The Committee suggests that a study of the sub-divisions of the four main aspects of social case work as presented in this report will reveal three categories into which the many items which collectively represent the subject matter of social case work can be assembled. They are:

(a) Factors in social case work which are well established, uniformly understood by social case workers and applied in practice with a fair degree of precision.

(b) Factors which are tentatively established, not clearly conceived but clearly apparent in practice.

(c) Factors which are apparent in practice but unsupported by clear formulations and which have thus far not been intellectually explored.

PART II

WHAT IS GENERIC SOCIAL CASE WORK?

INTRODUCTORY STATEMENT

The marks by which a professional service is distinguished from other professional services are its field, its objectives, its vocational resources and its characteristic methods of work. Social case work is a part of the professional service of social work. This report does not attempt to analyze the professional aspects of social work as a whole. It does attempt to present descriptions of the aspects of social case work as one division of social work. The arrangement of the discussion of generic social case work is analytical. Any one section will give only a partial impression unless it is read in relation to the others, especially Chapter XI. The Committee has avoided any attempt at definition because it doubts whether there is any substantial value in a definition of so complex a thing as a professional activity and because it believes that at the present stage of its development no definition of social case work can distinguish it sufficiently from other professional fields.

What is generic social case work? Its content can be conceived of as embodying the following aspects:

1. Knowledge of typical deviations from accepted standards of social life.
2. The use of norms of human life and human relationships.
3. The significance of social history as the basis of particularizing the human being in need.
4. Established methods of study and treatment of human beings in need.
5. The use of established community resources in social treatment.
6. The adaptation of scientific knowledge and formulations of experience to the requirements of social case work.
7. The consciousness of a philosophy which determines the purposes, ethics and obligations of social case work.
8. The blending of the foregoing into social treatment.

The elaboration of these aspects forms the body of Part II: What Is Generic Social Case Work? It is presented as the result of the effort to suggest the field, the objectives, the vocational resources and the methods of social case work.

The analysis of items under each section is not complete but is meant to be illustrative only. The method by which the Committee arrived at this particular list of items is indicated in Chapter II, pages 6-8.

CHAPTER IV
DEVIATIONS

Social case work deals with the human being whose capacity to organize his own normal social activities may be impaired by one or more deviations from accepted standards of normal social life of which the following are typical:

alcoholism
bad housing
bigamy
casual labor
child labor
child marriage
common law marriage
communicable disease
crime
delinquency
dependent old age
dependent orphanhood
dependent widowhood
destructive and
    unconstructive behavior
drug addiction
family antagonisms
family dependency
family desertion
foreignness
homelessness
illegitimacy

illiteracy
instability
insufficient wage
lack of skill in trade
mental ill health
migrancy
non-conformity
non-support
over-crowding
over-indulgence
parental neglect
pauperism
physical handicap
physical ill health
prostitution
seasonal employment
subnormal mentality
truancy
unemployment
unprotected childhood
vagrancy

There is not necessarily failure in self-maintenance when an individual is, for example, ill, unemployed, or financially dependent. These deviations have for social case work the significance of symptoms as well as causes. Social case work is concerned with these deviations because of their implications for the human being in whose life or experience they are present. Their leading implication for social case work is their relation to the possible impairment of the capacity of the individual to organize his own normal social activities. The functioning of this capacity we can call self-maintenance. There is failure in self-maintenance when the individual is unable to find his way out of his difficulties as a result of his own planning for himself. We suggest that the distinguishing concern of social case work is the capacity of the individual to organize his own normal social activities in a given environment.

The presence of these deviations does not necessarily suggest the need for the service of a social case worker any more than a minor ailment necessarily suggests a need for the service of a physician. They do suggest, how-ever, in any case, a need for some of the knowledge regarding these symp-toms and their causes which is part of the professional equipment of the social case worker just as even a minor ailment suggests, on behalf of the person who is ill, the importance of some degree of medical knowledge. This distinction is important first because it is neither necessary nor desirable that every human being should seek professional aid whenever any one or more of these deviations presents itself in his experience. They represent crises which, to a large extent, must be handled by the intelligence and common sense of the individuals concerned. They suggest a need for the service of social case work only when their presence or persistence implies impairment of the capacity for self-maintenance.

Self-maintenance is always relative to a given setting. The individual's capacity for it may be adequate in a rural environment, inadequate to the de-mands of city life, and the reverse is also true. It may be adequate in an old world setting and inadequate to the requirements of adjustment in a new country. Furthermore, complete self-maintenance in the sense in which we are using the term is not achieveable by children or by some of the chronically handicapped. In setting self-maintenance, therefore, as the objective of social case work with children and some of the chronically handicapped, we are us-ing it in a relative sense as applying only to that degree of self-maintenance which society expects from such persons.

Deviations from normal social life are, as symptoms, not the concern of social case work exclusively. Most of them come within the province of other professions, of industry or of the state, but with a different significance for each. Ill health, for example, is one of the primary concerns of the medical profession, but it has professional significance for social case work, even though social case work does not undertake the treatment of ill health for the patient. These deviations suggest a further point of contact between professions in that different professional services may be combined in the treatment of individual cases. Delinquency, for example, is primarily the responsibility of the Court. The successful treatment of the delinquent, how-ever, frequently requires the combined service of law, medicine, and social case work.

The most significant contribution of social case work to society is not its ability to deal with parental neglect, illiteracy, mental defect, physical handi-cap, pauperism and other items on the foregoing list but in its increasing ability to deal with the human being's capacity for self-maintenance when it has become impaired by these and other deviations from accepted standards of normal social life. It has made its highest contribution when its client no longer needs the social case worker, not because he no longer faces these deviations but because his developed capacity for self-maintenance is equal to the task of dealing with them unaided by a social case worker.

CHAPTER V
NORMS

Concepts of desirable social activities in individual lives are based upon certain norms of human life and human relationship. Among the norms for social case work are those associated with:

aesthetics	nationality
education	parenthood
family	personality
food, shelter, etc.	protected childhood
health, physical and mental	recreation
home	religion
justice	security
kinship	self-support
law	sex
literacy	social behavior
marriage	sociality
mutual advancement	voluntary associations
mutual protection	work

A recognition by social case work of norms of human life and human relationships is implied in its concepts of deviations and of social treatment. In all the procedures of social case work—selection of cases, diagnosis, treatment, closing of cases, evaluation of results—the practitioner has norms more or less clearly in mind. Without such a use of norms purposeful activity is hardly possible.

So far as we know the norms which are used in social case work have not been defined. We do not believe that at the present time they can be accurately defined or that any definition of them would be accepted generally. Furthermore, it is recognized that the word "norm" is used in different senses. It may connote a type or pattern which has evolved in nature or social life, or it may connote a standard which has been formulated as the deliberate product of human thought. In the first sense the norms which seem to us significant for social case work have been borrowed from other sciences, notably from biology. In the second sense, some of our most significant norms are taken from the mores of the times and some have been evolved or adapted by social case work for its specific needs.

We believe that the conceptions of the norms which are of importance in social case work must always be flexible and subject to differences of definition. Nevertheless, we believe that, at the present time, social case workers are more conscious of the existence of these norms than they are concretely aware of their implications. While social case workers may never

achieve exactitude or precision in the definition of the working norms of
social case work, we believe that a greater approach to exactitude and precision
is possible and that the need for this approach defines one important field of
study for social case workers with respect to their own problems. This is to a
considerable extent a philosophical problem. When progress has been made
in formulating the philosophy of social case work (See Part II, Chapter X,
page 28), much of it will be found illuminating in regard to working norms.

CHAPTER VI

PARTICULARIZATION OF THE INDIVIDUAL

The particularization of concepts of normal life and activities and of deviations from them may be accomplished with reference to individual persons in concrete situations by means of knowledge of such facts as the following:

1. *History*

Dates and places of births, marriages, deaths of individual members of family group; causes of death

Date of coming to U. S.; previous and present residences; citizenship; legal settlement

Education: school grades reached; special training

Social service exchange data; records of other agencies

Court records

Health records: statements from physicians, clinics, hospitals which have known any of group as to physical or mental illness or handicaps

Developmental history: age of dentition, etc., of members of family

Background

    family
    racial (national)
    cultural
    educational—school records past and present
    religious or church affiliation
    industrial—work records past and present
    recreation and special interests

Analysis of social difficulties

Previous plans of treatment

Response to treatment activities

2. *Current Personal Data*

Marital status

Social status

Income: sources

Budget

Debts

Resources

Usual occupation and weekly wage

Relationships
> within family group—husband and wife, parents and children, and children to each other
> with relatives
> with employers and fellow workers
> with friends and neighbors
> with teachers and fellow pupils

Radical changes in reaction to environment

Personality data
> habits of individual
>> in day-to-day living, eating, sleeping, drinking, etc.
>>> re: health
>>>> work
>>>> play
>>>> education
>>>> **sex**
>>>> religious observances
> attitudes of individual
> evidences or lack of social responsibility
> evidences or lack of individual responsibility
> ambitions
> choice of companions
> appearance
> interests
> abilities; disabilities
> likes; dislikes

3. *Current Environmental Data*

Housing: number of rooms; rent; condition of house; sleeping conditions; ventilation; light; cleanliness, etc.; condition of neighborhood
Community facilities or lacks
Church
Place of work, trade or occupation
School
Groupal relationships: clubs, labor unions, fraternal and other groups
Racial or national characteristics of neighborhood
Conflicts due to racial or national differences
Standing in the community
Reversals in financial status
Radical changes in general environment
Significant changes in neighborhood or location
Standards of living
> manners
> general atmosphere
> general attitudes of members of family toward one another
> relatives—attitude toward family or individual attitude toward discipline
> presence or lack of family group activities
> interest in housekeeping and home standards

We have already stated that development of the individual's capacity to organize his own normal social activities when this capacity has become impaired is the leading objective of social case work. Social case work deals with human beings one at a time. Treatment is possible only when generalizations regarding human personality and its capacities, and regarding deviations from accepted standards of normal social life, have been particularized for the individual concerned. Face to face with a client, a social case worker's first interest is to determine as accurately as possible his client's present condition with respect to self-maintenance, the factors which have been responsible for it and the resources available within him and to him which may be used in the process of helping him to a better adjustment.

This particularization is achieved by the social case worker in large measure through the social case history. A social case history is the social case worker's chart on the basis of which his treatment is planned. Nowhere in our analysis of social case work does its essential unity appear more strikingly than in the comparison of the range of social history which is considered important by the different specific fields. The foregoing list is intended to include all of the data now regarded as relevant by the various fields of social case work. The most striking fact regarding this compilation of data is its complete relevancy for each field of social case work, however much variation there may be at present in the social history outlines which the different fields use. The organizations in the field of social case work attach different degrees of emphasis to the same items in the list. There is no item, however, which would be regarded as of no significance by any one field.

CHAPTER VII

METHODS

In order to assist the individual to develop his capacity to organize his own normal social activities, social case work makes use of the following methods:

adoption	organization
after-care	participation
analysis	planning
case decision	prognosis
commitment	re-education
diagnosis	refer
evaluation	relief allowance
first interview	supervision
institutional care	transfer
integration of plans	transportation
interviewing	treatment
investigation	use of documents
observation	

This list of methods used in social case work is not complete. It has, however, been prepared after careful consideration of the best of social case work literature and by a committee whose members are aware of the current practices of social case workers. We believe that every item on the foregoing list has a definite technical connotation. We believe, furthermore, that with respect to all of these items this connotation becomes constantly more definite and more precise. Still further, we believe it to be true that while some of the methods on this list are used more often in some fields of social case work than in others, there is no item on the list which any social case worker, regardless of the field in which he is working, would think irrelevant for his purposes. In other words, it is in the growing body of method that we find one of the distinguishing marks of social case work as a professional field.

There is here no room for complacency, however. A glance at the foregoing list reveals the fact that the content of some of these methods is much more substantial than that of others. Social case workers are more sure-footed in their use of adoption, of the interview, of investigation, of the relief allowance, for example, than they are in the use of diagnosis, evaluation, and participation.

As a stimulus to discussion, the Committee presents the following definitions of some of the items in the hope that the difficulty of defining the content of social case work methods and of adding to the list may be accepted by social case workers as a problem requiring immediate and persistent study:

Analysis of data involves the sifting of relevant from irrelevant data, the assembling of material with reference to its significance and its arrangement with reference to the use that is to be made of it.

Case Discussion suggests the study by a group of competent persons of a case problem for the purpose of arriving at a definite formulation of desirable next steps.

Commitment is a definite method involving well-established steps by which an individual is placed in an institution or in the care of an agency which assumes formal responsibility for him.

Diagnosis is the method by which the social case worker reasons through a mass of assembled data to conclusions in terms of the problem toward which these data point. After the gathering of the social history, an attempt is made to formulate a diagnostic summary by this method. The process of diagnosis, however, is a continuous one and is used whenever the worker is trying to establish the significance of information secured.

Interviewing is the method through which most of the information used in social case work is secured and through which most of its results used in treatment are insured. Among the important aspects of interviewing in social case work are an alertness by the interviewer for leads to information which can be followed without antagonizing the person interviewed, the establishment of a relationship through the interview which will insure whole-hearted co-operation and an ability to cover as much ground as possible in as little time as possible without sacrificing the essential requirements of the relationship between the person interviewed and the organization.

Observation as a method in social case work involves a trained ability to detect significant facts without questioning.

Organization is an unsatisfactory term for the method by which a skilled worker directs his activities so that diagnosis, prognosis and plans come to fruition. It suggests both a habit of work and a relationship to other strategic persons which results in getting things done.

Participation is a name used to designate the method of giving to a client the fullest possible share in the process of working out an understanding of his difficulty and a desirable plan for meeting it.

Planning is a method which puts into social case work both an economy and an effective concentration of effort. It precedes every important step taken by the worker. Plans which are reduced to writing provide an important check on the adequacy of steps taken later.

Prognosis is a method adapted from the medical field by which a social case worker estimates the possibility of achieving a result with the problem in hand. It takes the form of suggesting that in the light of the situation as defined, if certain things specifically stated happen or can be made to happen a result in specifically stated terms is probable.

Use of Documents as a method in social case work involves an ability to prepare records having a maximum usefulness for a specific purpose and an ability to use documents and other forms of record scientifically.

Apparently social case workers are constantly becoming aware of new methods. We say "becoming aware" advisedly because we do not believe that the methods of social case work thus far recognized have been invented by them. They have rather used well-established methods of dealing with human beings, developed them for their own ends and by constant practice have given them technical significance. In the same way, without question, they will become aware of still other methods which they are now using effectively though perhaps less consciously.

The Committee believes that the recognition by social case workers of all fields, of the same fundamental methods provides the most substantial evidence of the common ground of social case work and an important justification for the belief of the Milford Conference that there is such a thing as generic social case work.

CHAPTER VIII

COMMUNITY RESOURCES FOR SOCIAL CASE WORK

The practice of social case work in behalf of persons whose capacity to organize their own normal social activities may be impaired involves effective relationships with various community resources outside the immediate field of social case work, such as the following:

churches	schools
courts	social agencies for education, rec-
industry	reation, law enforcement, and
insurance societies	the promotion of social and
medical agencies	health work
public departments	social legislation

To be completely suggestive, this list should be itemized to indicate the precise use which is made of these community resources as distinguished from the use made of these same resources in other forms of work. Such an itemization, however, the Committee found difficult. This difficulty perhaps suggests another point at which social case workers have not done sufficiently clear thinking and which ought, therefore, to be made a subject of persistent study.

In connection with this list of community resources, it should be noted that other types of community agencies may develop a point of contact with social case work. Within comparatively recent months, such contacts have been made, for example, between some fields of social case work and the American Legion, the safety movement, and the newly organized Cleanliness Institute, none of which perhaps can be well classified under any of the foregoing headings.

CHAPTER IX
ADAPTATION OF SCIENCE AND EXPERIENCE

For the understanding of its problems and the development of sound procedures for the accomplishment of its purposes, social case work draws upon a body of knowledge formulated from the data of its own experience and adapted from other organized fields of activity and from established sciences. This body of knowledge will include in part adaptations from the following:

biology	medicine
economics	psychiatry
education	psychology
law	sociology

The future growth of social case work is in large measure dependent upon its developing a scientific character. Its scientific character will be the result in part of a scientific attitude in social case workers towards their own problems and in part of increasingly scientific adaptations from the subject matter of other sciences, such as those mentioned in the foregoing list. Nowhere, so far as we know, has anybody attempted to formulate the concepts and factual material of science and other organized fields of activity which social case workers have adapted to their own ends. Such terms in constant use by social case workers as income, standard of living, heredity, behavior, motivation, budget, nutrition, mental tests, are not only terms which they have borrowed but each connotes an important concept and an impressive area of fact of which social case workers have made specific and technical use. It is relatively simple to record the fact of this appropriation of subject matter but it is exceedingly difficult at the present time to indicate the precise range of such subject matter and the nature of its technical use by social case work. Here again we suggest an important problem for study and research by social case workers. The first step in developing more substantial scientific training for social case workers is a more penetrating analysis by social case workers themselves of the scientific aspects of social case work.

CHAPTER X
PHILOSOPHY

Inherent in the practice of social case work is a philosophy of individual and social responsibility and of the ethical obligations of the social case worker to his client and to the community. Such concepts of responsibility must direct the use of all methods referred to in Chapter VII, and influence the relationships with community resources indicated in Chapter VIII. Moreover the idea of norm and deviation developed in Chapters IV and V, resting as it does upon "accepted standards" and "desirable social activities," suggests that we can perceive social values, plus and minus, in certain situations, and by these values justify our objectives in social case work.

The social case worker has need of a thought-out system of social values not only to clarify his general purpose and orient him in relation to theories of social progress, but also to guide him in every professional contact. Such practical questions as the following illustrate the need of a philosophy:

What are the client's rights as an individual?
What are his obligations to his family?
Under what circumstances is it good to try to maintain a family as such unbroken?
Under what circumstances is it good to try to break up a family? (i.e., What values are involved for individual, group, society?)
Is coercion justified in any given case?
How far and when is individual dependency a public responsibility, how far and when a private responsibility?
What individual social needs other than subsistence are public responsibility: education; health examination; mental test; vocational guidance; recreation; etc.?
How far should social environment be altered in the interest of the sick or unadjusted person?
In what circumstances, if any, should the client's confidence be violated by the social case worker?
Is the social case worker responsible for law enforcement?

Thus far the philosophy of social case work has been comparatively little discussed and hardly at all defined. We can at this point do no more than to record an awareness of its importance. We suggest again that discussion and formulation of the philosophy of social case work is a pressing obligation upon the members of the profession.

CHAPTER XI
SOCIAL CASE TREATMENT

The social case worker comes into the life of the client when his deviations from normal social standards have reached a point where he cannot effectively organize certain of his own activities. The measure of the skill of the social case worker is not only the body of knowledge and method he has acquired but his ability to utilize these creatively in social case treatment which has as its objectives the social well being of the client.

The goals of social case treatment are both ultimate and proximate. The ultimate goal is to develop in the individual the fullest possible capacity for self-maintenance in a social group. In attaining both immediate and ultimate goals three fundamental processes interplay at every point: (1) the use by the social case worker of resources—educational, medical, religious, industrial—all of which have a part in the adjustment of the individual to social living; (2) assisting the client to understand his needs and possibilities; and (3) helping him to develop the ability to work out his own social program through the use of available resources.

Proximate goals may involve such things as restoration of health; reestablishment of kinship ties; removal of educational handicaps; improvement of economic condition; overcoming of delinquent tendencies. The attainment of these goals, however, must be in such a way as to further not only the immediate but the ultimate well being of the client. For the social case worker to assume responsibilities which can and should be carried by the client will interfere with or make impossible the attainment of the ultimate goal of self-maintenance. On the other hand, if objectives are introduced into the treatment program at too early a stage for the client's assimilation there may be an equally serious negation of the ultimate purpose. For instance, where a client is suffering from severe economic need recognition and relief of this need by the social case worker is essential before mutual understanding can be established. Effective treatment likewise demands that the social case worker shall be able to guage the tempo and ability of the client in assuming responsibility—either to underestimate or to overestimate this ability is equally disastrous.

We could list the "treatment services" given on the statistical cards used by social case work agencies but they would give merely the bare bones of what is involved in social case treatment. The flesh and blood is in the dynamic relationship between social case worker and the client, child or foster parent; the interplay of personalities through which the individual is assisted to desire and achieve the fullest possible development of his personality. Social case treatment has to do with the way in which the social worker counsels with human beings; at every step it ties up with his understanding of those requiring service, with his concepts of social relationships and with his philosophy of normal standards of social life.

Nowhere does the fact that social case work is an art appear more clearly than in treatment. Here there is the blending of scientific knowledge, training and experience as in the finished picture. Here, too, the vision of the artist is made an actuality through his ability to combine in effective use— not only with skill but with genius—the separate units of his knowledge. But the social case worker has no passive canvas on which to paint his picture. The client himself must be a participant in the art of social case work.

In our discussion of methods we have defined participation as "the method of giving to a client the fullest possible share in the process of working out an understanding of his difficulty and a desirable plan for meeting it." In the family field, for example, and in large measure in the other fields, participation begins with the first contact between social case worker and client and continues to the end. It is an essential ingredient of interviewing (see page 24), of diagnosing, of planning and of the carrying out of plans. The philosophy of participation is more easily understood than is the method of achieving it. The method becomes in each individual case a working out of a philosophic concept in terms of an individual relationship.

As we go through the list of services which may be used to enable the client to organize his own social activities we find in each instance that participation by the client must be assumed. Take for example, "Employment secured" where the deviation from which the client is suffering is unemployment. The finding of a position for a man is but a small part of the picture— the rest is his willingness to undertake it plus his capacity, fitness and so on. Or, where the deviation is ill health, "clinic treatment" suggests not merely leading a patient to a dispensary, but an awakening in him of a desire to seek examination and to participate in the prescribed medical treatment. "Family reunited"—another service item—implies far more than bringing together a family group under one roof. It suggests a state of mind in the family-client, an awareness on the part of its members of the social and individual values of such a reunion and an acceptance by them of the task of satisfactorily working out the relationships within the group. All of these attitudes must be developed through the participation of client and social case worker.

Likewise in the children's field, in the field of the visiting teacher, and in medical social work, where often the social case worker-client relationship is less prominent, the influence of one personality upon another is still a potent factor in treatment. For example, the children's visitor to a foster home may for quite satisfactory reasons not see the child on a given visit, and may prefer not to do so. It may be her purpose to awaken or strengthen in the foster parents desires to serve the needs of the child, so that through them there may develop within the child those latent capacities which the foster parent without the visitor would not have discovered or been patient or capable enough to cultivate. The methods in the various fields may be different, but the principle in treatment through the interplay of personalities applies to all.

It is not too much to say that effective social case treatment affects the social case worker as well as the client. A social case worker whose own personality development is not furthered through his contacts with his clients is probably not an effective social case worker.

It is the human but intangible and unmeasurable aspects of treatment which are the most important, and which offer the most genuine test of the social case worker's mastery of his art. "She gives me courage," said one woman in speaking of a social case worker. "I was thrilled to see courage and life flowing back into the discouraged mother," remarked a social case worker. Whence came this new power to face life with all its difficulties? Not merely from the removal of obstacles, nor from the social case worker alone, but from the creation of an effective relationship between the mother and her social world, an act of creation in which she herself shared or there would have been no revivifying contact with the current of life. The creative use of methods and knowledge which would otherwise be but mechanical tools gives color, warmth and vitality to that relationship between human beings which is the adventure of social case work.

PART III

WHAT IS A COMPETENT AGENCY FOR SOCIAL CASE WORK?

A competent social case work agency is one which meets the tests required by the following:

The maintenance of high standards of case work practice.

Acceptance of responsibility for the study of social case work: its problems, methods, and results.

The practice of sound principles of organization.

The acceptance of definite responsibility towards the community and the maintenance of effective community relationships.

Efficiency in the management of its personnel.

CHAPTER XII
STANDARDS OF SOCIAL CASE WORK PRACTICE

At its best social case work means the practice of generic social case work (See Part II) within the setting of a specific field. Social case work is carried on almost universally through the medium of organizations which with few exceptions represent a specialization in the field. There are no organizations for generic social case work, there are only specific agencies. The only exception to this would seem to be the undifferentiated case work agency of which, so far as the Committee knows, there are few at the present time. Moreover with the development of the field in which it operates the undifferentiated case work agency tends to develop either into a departmentalized agency on the basis of specialization in case work or to abandon certain of its functions to other agencies created for the purpose of performing them.

This application of the subject matter of generic social case work in a specific setting means chiefly the adaptation of the various concepts, facts and methods which we have discussed as generic social case work to the requirements of the specific field. It means in part also certain other subject matter supplementary to the content of generic social case work. The nature of both adaptations and supplementations will be determined by the peculiar and distinctive requirements of the specific fields. If we try to state these peculiar and distinctive requirements for any one field, they would seem to be in part a more intensive development of some aspect of generic social case work than is necessary in other fields and in part quite distinctive equipment, for which other fields have little use. An example of the former would be the development for practitioners in medical social work of medical knowledge beyond what is required in other fields. An example of the latter would be the ability to evaluate the essential qualities of a foster home which is a distinctive development of the children's field. Complete equipment for a specific field would include the following:

1. The full content of generic social case work.
2. The intensive development of appropriate aspects of generic social case work.
3. Distinctive subject matter for which other specific fields have little or no use.

We have selected for illustration a few of the specific fields of social case work and have secured from representatives of each lists of items covering peculiar and distinctive equipment of the third type suggested in the preceding paragraph.

SOME DISTINCTIVE REQUIREMENTS OF CERTAIN SPECIFIC FIELDS

A. Family Welfare

1. A knowledge of the minimum essentials for keeping a family together.
2. A knowledge of home management.
3. An ability to estimate the significance and to make use of the implications of different national cultures.
4. A knowledge of the effect of migrancy on family life, on individuals temporarily cut off from their families, etc.
5. A knowledge of the effect of permanent removal from one demographical setting to another.
6. An understanding of and ability to deal with the psychology of economic failure.
7. Skill in administration of relief to families.
8. An understanding of and ability to deal with the psychology of enforced idleness.
9. Special case work equipment for dealing with unemployed persons.
10. Adaptation of technique to meet large scale relief problems.

B. Child Welfare

1. A knowledge of the minimum essentials for keeping a family together.
2. A working knowledge of the laws and legal procedure relating to the legal custody and the rights of the child.
3. An understanding of the skillful use of coercion for the stabilization of the treatment of a children's case problem.
4. By training and experience a children's worker has
    (a) A better understanding of the values and limitations of a foster home as against the child's own home, and
    (b) the ability to secure an interpretation of her plans and results through the foster parents.
5. A successful children's worker has the ability to visualize and evaluate a potential foster home or institution and its contribution to a particular type of need.
6. In taking a long-range view of the child's life the children's worker emphasizes the protection and re-establishment of the child's parental and family relationships.
7. The children's worker acquires special capacity for understanding the use of stimuli and the interpretation of responses in children.

C. Visiting Teaching

1. Knowledge of the visiting teacher's place in the school as a whole and her relationship to the other administrative departments.
2. A knowledge of the psychology of the classroom teacher with respect to the problems and extra-mural relationships of pupils.
3. Recognition of the values and limitations of the use of the visiting teacher's connection with the school in her relationship with children and parents.
4. Ability to observe the child in class without calling attention to him or interrupting class work.

5. An ability to do concentrated work with a child as a member of a group without stigmatizing him in the eyes of the other members of the group.
6. An ability to deal with parental criticism of the school.
7. Knowledge of special school arrangements, such as graded classes, transfers, promotion, etc.
8. Ability to secure the co-operation of teachers in individualizing the teacher's work with the child through providing graded tasks for discouraged or timid children, etc.
9. Ability to interpret gradual or partial improvement to the teacher.
10. Ability to draft a record and record system which will be adapted to the requirements of the school and the attitudes of school authorities.

D. Medical Social Work

1. Medical-social diagnosis, based on analysis of inter-relationships, especially causal inter-relationships, between social and health factors in case situations.
2. Interpretation of No. 1 to other agencies and to the patient and the patient group.
3. Teamwork with physician in medical-social case study and treatment.
4. Social case practice within hospital organization (functioning as part of hospital).
5. Arrangement and management of convalescence.
6. Social case work with the physically handicapped, i.e., appliance use, work adjustment.
7. Provision for chronically sick and disabled (especially by admission to special institutions).
8. Protection of individuals and groups against communicable disease by
   (a) teaching principles and methods of protection to patient and patient group;
   (b) use of public health resources: laws, regulations, bureaus, departments, clinics, etc.
9. Promotion of hygiene and sanitation, by
   (a) teaching of patient and patient group;
   (b) use of public health resources.

E. Psychiatric Social Work

1. Ability to formulate psychiatric-social diagnosis and treatment steps based on an analysis of inter-relationships of clinical examinations and environmental factors in the social data, both symptomatic and causative, in the case situation.
2. Ability to formulate the social interpretation of the psychiatric, the psychological and the physical findings, and carry out the treatment, for any individual in the situation, controlled by appreciation of the motivation, causative factors, and the recipient's present ability to understand and assimilate this material. (Whether applied to a member of the patient's family or to school or other professional personnel, this is part of the treatment of the patient's situation.)
3. The ability to elucidate the problem stated in terms of symptomatic behavior and to gather significant social data in the form of a differential

history for the purpose of supplementing the psychiatric, psychological and physical examinations on a particular psychiatric problem.

4. Ability to assume direct responsibility for dealing with the personal attitudes and modifying the personal relationships which contribute to the psychiatric problem but which in the opinion of the clinical group are more readily susceptible to the psychiatric social worker's influence than to that of the psychiatrist.

5. Ability to formulate the application of psychiatric social work content to the professional activities of a non-psychiatric group.

6. Special orientation and ability necessary to interpret to an agency or an individual in the abstract or as part of case treatment, the function and scope of institutions concerned with custody and treatment of individuals with mental or personality deviations, i.e.: neuro-psychiatric hospitals, neuro-psychiatric clinics, institutions for the feebleminded, or courts where they are concerned with matters of commitment.

7. The ability to interpret to psychiatric clinical staff, effectively for the case, the functional potentialities of a participating, non-psychiatric agency, and that agency's need for comprehending the psychiatric problems and treatment indicated.

8. Ability to adapt psychiatric social work content to an educational program for the protection of the individual and the group against mental disease, delinquency, and socially unacceptable behavior.

Note: The psychiatric social worker may function in hospitals and social agencies of all types where special recognition is given to personality deviations. Her function varies from supplementing and participating in frankly superficial diagnostic work to active individual therapy on cases of social maladjustment.

F. Probation Work

1. A working knowledge of criminal law and procedure, and of law and procedure concerning juvenile delinquency and domestic relations.

2. Knowledge of the history and present application of all forms of penal treatment.

3. Knowledge of the social causes and conditions producing delinquency.

4. Understanding of the nature of group delinquency as found in gangs, and of the treatment necessary for the breaking up or conversion of these.

5. Understanding of the part played by abnormal mental states in producing crime or anti-social conduct.

6. The ability to make wise use of the authority of the court and the judicial discretion vested in the probation officer.

It would be difficult to get agreement on a complete list of the specific fields of social case work. In addition to the six just described, the status of specific field is given to parole, vocational guidance, work with homeless men, protective work with girls, and so forth. There is also a tendency to classify social case work in terms of institutions in connection with which it is done, e. g., social case work under governmental auspices, social case work in industry, social case work in the church, and so on. Within several of the specific fields mentioned there is a variety of agencies, such as Travelers Aid, American Red Cross, International Institute, International Migration Service, family welfare societies in the family field, and similar distinctions in the children's field. In such cases the name of the agency does not necessarily indicate the specific field.

Some of the items in the foregoing lists suggesting the distinctive equipment of specific fields may seem to be of the second type mentioned on page 35, "the intensive development of appropriate aspects of generic social case work," rather than of the third type, "distinctive subject matter for which other specific fields have little or no use." Among the items which may be of the second rather than the third type are:

1. A knowledge of the minimum essentials for keeping a family together.
2. Skill in administration of relief to families.
3. The children's worker acquires special capacity for understanding the use of stimuli and the interpretation of responses in children.
4. An ability to do concentrated work with a child as a member of a group without stigmatizing him in the eyes of the other members of the group.
5. Promotion of hygiene and sanitation.
6. Knowledge of the social causes and conditions producing delinquency.

Some of the lists also include items of procedure which are identical for several fields except for a specific adaptation; for example, "social case work practice" in hospitals, schools, courts, etc.

The development of social case work along specific lines calls for further comment in terms of the probable effect of specific practice as now organized upon generic social case work.

The work of this Committee developed out of a growing conviction among the members of the Milford Conference that there is a unity in the whole field of social case work regardless of its specific applications. The work of the Committee has confirmed its members in this conviction. We not only believe that the common ground of social case work is more extensive, more important, and more significant than its specific differences, but we believe that without exception the development of social case work has received and must continue to receive important contributions to its professional resources from each of these specific fields.

Nevertheless, there are important differences in the administrative status of family case work and children's case work on the one hand and those forms of social case work on the other which are carried on under the wing of other forms of activity. Most of the family and children's case work at the present time is carried on under its own auspices. The extent and the form of its service are determined by social case work leadership. Social case work in hospitals, in mental hygiene agencies, in schools, in courts, in industry, on the other hand, is carried on under the auspices of these other forms of work. In these fields, the extent and form of social case work service are determined by the requirements of other programs, medical, educational, legal, industrial.

There is in this distinction no suggestion of any difference in standards. There are, however, important differences in emphasis which are determined in part, at least, by the administrative requirements of programs which are not primarily the programs of social case work.

This difference in emphasis involves for generic social case work both value and risk. The establishment of social case work within the administrative areas of these other professions and under their administrative control has undoubtedly brought a rich contribution from these fields to social case work. On the other hand, there is the undoubted risk that this scattering of administrative control may foster a separatist tendency prejudicial to its unified development. The Committee believes that safeguards against any such separatist tendency lie in recognition of the paramount significance of generic social case work and in continuous contribution from all of its specific fields to its generally accepted body of knowledge and methods of work. The Committee records its conviction that the present acceptance of the full meaning of generic social case work is more widespread than is the interest in any separatist tendency on the part of social case workers.

The significance of this discussion for the maintenance of high standards in social case work practice is perhaps obvious. The safeguard of social case work against a separatist tendency evidently inherent in specialization lies in the continuous contribution of the specific fields towards the enrichment of the subject matter of generic social case work. At the same time the development of the subject matter of generic social case work must be so flexible as to permit of its easy adaptation to the requirements of specific fields. This gives every social case work agency a twofold responsibility in the matter of standards, a responsibility with respect to its own requirements and a further responsibility in respect to the growth, content and stability of social case work as such.

It is recognized that emergencies arise both in community life and in the experience of individual agencies. At such times good social case work practice demands that some of the requirements of a high standard of social case work be waived for the time being. This should not be construed as a lowering of standards but rather as evidence of a flexibility in standards which is essential to good social case work procedure.

CHAPTER XIII
The Study of Social Case Work

Whatever progress has been made in raising the standards of social case work has come about primarily because the case worker has had the capacity to learn through experience. When one works at an increasingly complex task, as social case workers do, continued practice is likely to result chiefly in a refinement of technique. The growth and development of a movement, however, depend more upon the influx of new ideas than upon the refinement of technique. New ideas are developed chiefly through study, although the study may be the study of one's own experience. For this reason, we believe that every social case work agency should be constantly analyzing its own problems and methods. Only by this process can it be sure of its own sound development. As we have pointed out in the introduction to this report, a leading impression made upon the members of the Committee by their discussion of social case work and its organization has been an impression of the vagueness of many of its most important concepts, of the meagerness of the elaboration of principles and of the ignorance of other important aspects of this professional field. All of this, as we have stated repeatedly, points to the imperative need for study and research in the field of social case work.

Who is to engage in this study and research? If its results are to be valid for social case work most of such research must be done by those who know social case work—in other words, social case workers—and all of it must be done in consultation at least with social case workers. It is quite possible that there may in time be established institutes for research in social case work analogous to institutes for medical research; indeed, some agencies, such as the Russell Sage Foundation, are now in part performing that function. A limited part of this task of research may be assumed by educational institutions. It seems to us, however, not only desirable but imperative that much of it be undertaken by the national and local social case work agencies themselves and by individual social case workers in their employ. We have already stated our hope that this report may serve the purpose of indicating many of the gaps in knowldege and equipment toward which such studies might be directed. We believe that nothing is more important for the progress of social case work during the next ten years than the production by social case workers and social case work agencies of documents of many kinds which would fill in these gaps and thereby make possible at the end of ten years an incomparably richer study of social case work than this Committee, at any rate, has been able to produce in 1928. Our emphasis is not wholly upon the importance of adding to the knowledge of the subject matter of social case work. The study of social case work as a mark of a competent agency is important also because the development of the habit of inquiry into the significance of their own experiences will in the long run contribute to a better qualified personnel for the practice of social case work itself.

We are not suggesting that every agency for social case work should have a department of research, although we see no reason why such a department should not be established by any agency if its resources permit. We do suggest that a part of the time and equipment of every agency should be devoted to such needs as an analysis of the total volume of its work, to the study of the increasingly complex problems presented to it, to the analysis of the persistent difficulties which it encounters in its practice, to those aspects of its work where its practice varies from the practice of other similar agencies. Such studies and others should be part of the regular program of every agency. Staff members should be given time to make them and volunteers should be used in connection with them. This general obligation rests upon national organizations quite as much as upon local societies. Indeed, it is in some ways more logical and possibly more practicable for the national organization, than for the local organization, to undertake research of a substantial character.

If social case workers are to extend their interest and activity in research it is suggested that three considerations need to be borne in mind:

1. A substantial amount of what is known of forces, factors, phenomena which affect human well being, has been acquired by the study of human beings whom they have affected adversely. Laboratory and statistical research are indispensable to an understanding of humanity and human welfare but they are not the whole of research. Clinical research, to borrow a phrase from the field of medicine, is indispensable. Social case workers come into contact daily with human beings whom the social environment has affected adversely. The exploration of this experience through research projects will add to the knowledge and method which together form the major part of the equipment of social case work for its function in modern life.

But the research of the social case worker should go beyond the discussing of data and principles necessary for the discharge of his own immediate function. It should aim to throw light upon deep-seated factors in social life which lead to difficulties of adjustment between the individual and his social environment. Unemployment, for example, as the social case worker encounters it, is usually a problem of the individual adjustment of the unemployed person through whatever measure of social treatment may be necessary. Unemployment is more than this, however: it is a widespread social problem which can neither be understood nor dealt with effectually except by many-sided research. Economists, social philosophers, political scientists, industrial experts have each a contribution to make. To this list should be added the social case worker whose peculiar responsibility towards unemployment as a broad social problem arises from his distinctive experiences in dealing in an intimate way with the adverse effects of unemployment upon human beings.

We have cited unemployment as an illustration only. Insofar as any broad social problem could be better understood and therefore more intelligently met by a study of the experience of social case work the responsibility for initiating such study must be assumed by social case work.

2. All of the foregoing discussion presents research as an ambitious program. Real research requires special skill, concentration and facilities; and work of this high character is urgently needed in social case work. It cannot be done scientifically except by social case workers who have also the special equipment and the time required. There is a vast difference between a research project and a study to secure data for publicity or for a propagandist report although the two are not necessarily incompatible.

This point is stressed because there is a widespread tendency to draw conclusions which are not supported by adequate data and to insist upon calling the process research. Social case workers have much to learn about the validity and efficiency of methods of social research. The first lesson is in the nature of the scientific method.

3. The final consideration to be borne in mind by case workers who take seriously the obligation to study social case work as well as to practice it is that there is urgent need of studies of problems and methods less ambitious in scope than research projects must be. Any social case worker who becomes aware of a recurring problem or difficulty may examine it, may begin to analyze his experience with it, may tabulate facts regarding it and find himself at the end of the process with at least a more intelligent attitude toward it and may even have a promising lead for its solution. If so, the study has been worth while and its results may be worth transmitting to others. Progress towards better standards, better methods, better understanding of social work is likely for a long time to come to be as dependent upon many such minor studies as these as it is upon the results of more formal research projects. The three essentials in such studies are a clear definition of the problem to be studied, accuracy in securing data and the restriction of conclusions to those which the data secured will support.

We recognize that we are proposing nothing new. Research and less ambitious studies which may not merit the label of research have always been undertaken by social case work agencies and no small part of present professional resources is the result of such efforts. Emphasis on this matter in this report is chiefly for the purpose of stimulating more widespread participation and of suggesting at least the possibility of a greater integration of research acivities through increasing consciousness by social case workers as a group of their own obligations.

As illustrations of studies which have been made by individual social case workers and groups and which have made a definite contribution to higher standards of social case work, we give the following list:

1. Success and Failure in the Promotion of Normal Life. A study of a selected group of closed cases of the United Charities of Chicago, made by Florence Nesbitt, published in *The Family,* December, 1926.

2. Study of the Use of the Church in a Congested District in Cleveland, made by Margaret Bailey, published in *The Family,* December, 1925.

3. Use of Recreation in Family Case Work. A study of a group of families in Cleveland, made by a Cleveland staff worker.

4. A Study of Tuberculous Families, made by Florence T. Waite, Cleveland, published in *The Family,* March, 1925.

5. Studies in Venereal Disease and Feeblemindedness, made by the New York Charity Organization Society, Social Research Department.

6. Study of Miner's Asthma in a Group of Families in Scranton Family Welfare Society.

7. The Working Relationship of Fifteen Case Working Agencies, made by Helen Wallerstein, Philadelphia, 1919.

8. Principles of Supervision and Relations Between Supervisors, formulated by the staff of the Los Angeles Travelers Aid Society, published in the *Newsletter* of the American Association for Organizing Family Social Work, January, 1928.

9. Travelers Aid Society—Its Contacts with Health Problems, by Margaret Wead, published by *Hospital Social Service,* Volume XVI, page 132.

10. A Follow-up Study of 550 Illegitimacy Applications, made by Ida R. Parker, Research Bureau for Social Case Work, 1924.

CHAPTER XIV
PRINCIPLES OF ORGANIZATION

We believe that certain principles of organization may be set up as inherent in competency as applied to a social case work agency. Among them may be listed the following:

1. In private agencies there should be a membership which elects the board of directors.
2. In all agencies, both public and private, there should be a functioning board (divided into classes whose terms of office expire in rotation) which holds regular meetings, preferably monthly.
3. The private society should be incorporated and should operate under the full endorsement of the appropriate State department, if such endorsement is provided for by State authority.
4. The private society should operate under a constitution and by-laws, defining its purposes and field of service but these should be so stated as to permit flexibility in the extension of its activities.
5. Every social case work agency, whether public or private, should issue an annual report to the community.
6. The functions of the board of directors should include the appointment of the chief executive officer, full financial responsibility and budgetary control, the formulation and approval of general policies and scrutinizing of the work of the organization by means of regular reports to the board from the chief executive officer and the participation of board members in committee work.
7. The function of the chief executive should include attendance at all board meetings, attendance in person or by a representative at all committee meetings, the preparation of agenda for board meetings in consultation with the president or a designated member of the board and full executive responsibility and authority within the general program for the organization laid down by the board.
8. The business affairs of the organization should be conducted in accordance with accepted business standards and practice, including the auditing of accounts at least annually by a certified public accountant.
9. It should be recognized that the quality as well as the quantity of the organization's service is definitely dependent upon the adequacy of its office facilities.

The foregoing principles constitute a general structure of competency with respect to organization in a social agency whose exclusive functions are those of social case work. Social case work under public auspices presents organization problems of its own, such as legislative restrictions upon field and scope of activity, administrative responsibility, civil service regulations, and so on. As we have indicated in our formulation of the foregoing principles, most of them seem to us to apply to social case work under public auspices and we think that in spirit all of them do.

When social case work is a department of an organization whose chief function is not social case work, such as the hospital, the school or the court, the organization problem is quite different. Even here, however, we believe that many of the foregoing principles apply. Recognizing the special problem of social case work as a department of other agencies, we present the following suggestions concerning the organization and administration of "mural" social case work.

ORGANIZATION AND ADMINISTRATION OF "MURAL" SOCIAL CASE WORK

The Committee uses the term "mural" to designate social case work carried on in institutions the primary purpose of which is the practice of some other profession, such as education, law, or medicine. Children's institutions at the present stage in their development seem to share in the use of the term "mural case work." But a more careful study of the application of case work to children's institutions leads us to believe that the use of the institution is to become a part of the social case work process in the same way as the use of the foster home has become a recognized part, a relationship which is being increasingly achieved in modern children's institutions. The school, the court, and the hospital, on the other hand require social case work to complete their primary professional services and fulfill their purposes, and in each of these institutions social case work becomes for the time being a part of the practice of another profession, the purpose of which it serves according to its competency as social case work.

Two major principles must be recognized in the organization and administration of "mural" social case work, namely, (1) integration of the institution, and (2) maintenance of professional standards. It will help to avoid conflict of these two principles if the administrative machinery of the institution is thought of as existing for the purpose of enabling the professional services to function. Integration of the institution may therefore be secured by clear allocation of administrative responsibilities and relationships, while at the same time the several associated services thus administered are left free to follow the principles and techniques each of its own professional leaders. Responsibility for maintenance of professional standards thus rests in each instance with the head (individual or committee) of the department, who is nevertheless administratively responsible to the superintendent of the institution and through him to the board of trustees or governmental department which is the repository of the community's interest in the institution.

The organization of the hospital, for example, provides for a professional body to set and maintain professional standards for the primary professional service, but does not provide any corresponding professional supervisory group for the social and other services. This is approximately true, *mutatis mutandis,* of other institutions such as school and court. The relatively simple organization of the social service and its secondary position in the institution in relation to the medical service make it reasonable that the head of the department should embody final professional responsibility.

It is, however, important that department heads have access to the support and guidance of their own professional groups. This access may be provided by membership in local and national professional organizations, and by the right and obligation to come under the supervision of committees and commissions, private or governmental, such as the National Probation Association and the National Committee on Visiting Teaching.

It is important also that the professional services within each institution be correctly related to the community. In general, a board of trustees or a governmental department represents the institution to the community and the community to the institution. In order to perfect the relationships of each service, the board or governmental department may well organize special advisory committees, either among the board or department members, or from other interested citizens. If the committee is organized from outside citizens, some of its members should sit as representatives of the committee upon the governing board.

Such an advisory committee may perform an important double function. On the one hand it brings to the department the stimulus of the special interest of the community in its particular service and supports with the strength of the community the interest of the department. On the other hand the committee serves as a means of educating the community as to the meaning of the service and thereby develops a supporting group which makes increasingly enlightened requirements of and for the service.

While this applies to all services of an institution, it seems particularly applicable to social case work, because the community itself is so largely the object of social study and treatment.

The professional inter-relationships of the services within the institution tend to require some structuralization or building into the organization. Professional services may accomplish a measure of integration through interlocking advisory committees and through full representation on the board of trustees.

These principles we believe are emerging, although in actual fact organization of such working inter-relationships is in an early and experimental stage, and varies much from institution to institution.

CHAPTER XV
COMMUNITY RESPONSIBILITIES AND RELATIONSHIPS

Part I of this report discussed generic social case work as restricted to the practice of the social case work agency with respect to its clients. The full responsibility of the social case work agency, however, goes far beyond this. It has certain obligations towards the community, the discharge of which in the long run is essential to good social case work but which have significance also in other ways than those concerned with the relationship of the agency to its clients.

We believe that the competent social case work agency should limit its intake, its activities and the geographical area within which it operates in whatever ways may be necessary in order to maintain sound standards of social case work practice and effective community relationships. This limitation of intake, activities and area must be determined by local considerations in force at any given time. No agency, however, should spread itself out so thin as to prevent the maintenance of high standards of work except when such a practice is dictated by an emergency. No agency should preempt so large a portion of the community problem or so large a geographical area as to prevent the development of other agencies when the total problem is apparently beyond its own resources. The spreading of resources so thin as to prevent good social case work may be the wise policy to pursue in individual situations for locally strategic reasons. It should be recognized, however, that an agency which persistently holds to this policy is not a competent agency.

This should not be interpreted as meaning that a social case work agency should concern itself only with that part of the local problems of its field which it can handle efficiently. On the contrary, we believe that every social case work agency has an obligation towards the total community problem in its own field. As we have just indicated, this obligation may in emergencies express itself in a willingness to do inadequate work. It should more normally express itself, however, in an effort to secure adequate resources for its own program or in stimulating the development of additional agencies in order to make the community equipment commensurate with its need.

A competent social case work agency has a responsibility for the use of its knowledge of social factors contributing to the maladjustment of individuals and families so as to bring about a modification of these unfavorable conditions. Whenever the experience of a social case worker provides convincing evidence that the maladjustment of human beings is either caused by or persists because of the defective functioning of any social machinery the agency has an obligation to make this evidence known and do whatever it can, without prejudicing its own usefulness, to stimulate efforts to remedy such conditions.

A further mark of competency in a social case work agency is such a relationship with other agencies as will enable them all to further their own objectives and enable them to decide upon a desirable division of labor in their own communities.[1] It is pertinent to comment here that a successful division of labor among case work agencies of a community implies an attitude of free and fruitful conference whenever the occasion arises. As is pointed out in Part IV, some social case work problems are so intricate and at some points the functions of the specialized agency are necessarily so difficult to define that over and over again differences of opinion will arise which cannot be reconciled by any logical principles. In such instances, the only recourse is to a conference undertaken with the expectation (not merely the hope) that a satisfactory working solution of the immediate issue can be found. Nothing will so completely insure the success of such conferences as the continuous maintenance by an agency of relationships with other agencies based upon common recognition of a common stake in the total problem of the community.

We believe further that the competent social case work agency has a responsibility to contribute to the effectiveness of any state-wide facilities for joint expression regarding the findings, the needs, and the experiences of the community's social work.

We believe further that social work has become a unified national movement. This implies that progress in social work in the local community is stimulated by the interplay of a local society with the kindred national movement with which it is affiliated. The value of such relationship is twofold and reciprocal. The vitality that comes to the local society through intelligent sharing of its experience with other communities in turn helps the national movement to bring assistance to the local society through the promotion of efforts, through criticism and the interpretation of standards and through facilitating inter-agency contacts.

As a final phase of the community responsibility of the competent agency, we suggest its obligation to develop and strengthen in every possible way the participation of laymen in social case work. Since social case work in its present form of organization is dependent in high degree both upon the financial support and upon the community influence of its lay participants, its standards cannot maintain an advance beyond the point of the layman's recognition of their value. The more complex social problems appear and the more highly developed the skill which their solution requires, the more important does it become that the intelligence of the community outside of social work be aware both of the complexity of the problems and the na-

---

[1]The problem of the division of labor is discussed in detail in Part IV of this report.

ture of the skill required to deal with them. It may be questioned whether, in the long run, these facts will be accepted by the community solely on the statement of the professional social worker. Conviction on the part of the intelligeht public regarding social case work and its needs must rest not merely on the revelations and the arguments of the professional worker but also upon the experience of the layman gained in actual participation.

The argument for lay participation goes deeper than this. In the last analysis the purposes, the objectives and the values in the service of social case work are not created by the professional worker; they are the product of the social philosophy of the community. Not what social case workers think can be done with or in behalf of those persons who have deviated from accepted standards of social life but what the citizenship of the community wishes the quality of its community life to be will determine the scope and character of its social work. As an expert, the social worker should be able to tell his community the truth regarding its social problems. He should be able also to suggest what can be done about such problems. As a member of the community, he should have also a valid judgment as to how much of this program of what could be done is desirable and is in line with the highest human purposes. At this point, however, the motives, the experience and the philosophy of others than experts in social work are as valid as his own. In a sound formulation, therefore, of purposes, objectives and policies in social case work, the contribution of the layman is indispensable.

At the present time the development of social case work is in a transition stage. Less than two generations ago the earlier stages of social case work were guided and controlled by laymen. Within the past three or four decades the professional worker has steadily taken over almost all aspects of social case work practice which were formerly in the hands of laymen. From a narrow point of view this is the inevitable development of every form of service in which expertness has been or can be developed. It is perhaps not unnatural that the full momentum of this development should have crept upon social case workers unawares although there is plenty of evidence that laymen at least have been uncomfortably conscious of it for some time past. If, as we have pointed out, lay participation is indispensable both to the permanence of social work in the community and its sound development, it would seem to be an obligation upon the competent social case work agency to find ways whereby the participation of laymen can be increased. We do not believe that this should involve the curtailment of the responsibility or the authority of the expert. We believe that when social case workers have given as much attention to this problem as they have to some problems in the development of their own expertness as social case workers the way will be open to the joint participation of expert and laity in the pursuit of their common objective.

CHAPTER XVI
PERSONNEL

Efficiency in the management of personnel will characterize the competent agency in social case work. For some reasons the dependence of professional standards upon qualified personnel presents greater difficulties to social work than to other professions. As compared with medicine, the ministry, law and probably teaching, social work is much less well-equipped with programs for professional education, with professional organization and technical literature. Professional education, professional organization and technical literature are powerful reinforcements of the stability of any profession. Except for the native ability of the practitioner, they together constitute the most important single medium for the development of professional standards. Lacking anything like adequate resources on these three points, the reliance of social case work for high standards in practice must be upon the two factors of organization and personnel. The efficiency of each of these factors depends largely upon the personnel practices of social case work agencies. The success of the agency in meeting its obligations to its public is in the hands of its staff. The professional development of social case workers which, in the long run, determines the standards of social case work, is largely influenced by the administrative setting provided for them by social case work agencies.

Personnel management has within recent years become a matter of close study. Social case work is one form of activity which has contributed, along with industry and other fields, to the understanding of the problem. Here, again, however we approach a problem of social case work for which our awareness is much more nearly adequate than our understanding. We suggest, nevertheless, that the experience of social case workers in the management of personnel has proved the validity of some important principles.

These, we believe, can be divided into three categories, involving:

1. Aspects of the relationship between agency and employee which should be matters of contract.
2. Aspects of the relationship between agency and employee which have a basis in professional ethics and are of the nature of professional privileges to be accorded the employee and of professional obligation on the part of the employee to the organization beyond those things which should be embodied in a contract.
3. Methods of conducting staff relationships so as to insure the efficiency of the organization through the safeguarding of the privileges and obligations discussed under No. 2.

(51)

ITEMS OF CONTRACT BETWEEN THE WORKER AND THE AGENCY

We are assuming that an agency has a definite routine for the selection of employees which gives it an adequate basis for judging the qualifications of candidates. Every employee of a social case work agency should have a written statement which defines the duties of the position to which he is appointed as precisely as possible, the length of the period for which he is employed, the salary he is to receive, the hours during which he is expected to be on duty and the length of his annual vacation. It has been found desirable by many agencies to include as a condition of engagement that employees submit to regular physical examination, usually not less often than once a year. There is also a growing interest in the possibility of including in the contractual relationship between agency and employee provision for a pension or other allowance upon retirement.

Positions in social case work under public auspices are usually covered by civil service regulations which are in the nature of a contract between the government and its employees. The complete set of regulations covering any one position or any type of position in the public service being fixed by legislation is ordinarily less flexible than the contractual practices of a private agency need be. Nevertheless we believe that all of the items which we have suggested as desirable in the contract between the private agency and its employees should be included in the civil service arrangements for positions in social case work under governmental auspices.

The termination of the contractual relationship between a competent agency and its employees involves obligations on both sides. An agency which wishes to terminate this relationship is under obligation to give its employee adequate notice. At the termination of the relationship on the initiative of an agency, a social case worker is entitled to receive from the agency, confidentially if he desires it, an exact statement of the reasons for the termination. When the relationship is terminated on the initiative of a worker, the obligation to give the agency ample notice is exactly the same as that which rests upon the agency when it takes the initiative.

THE PROFESSIONAL PRIVILEGES OF THE SOCIAL CASE WORKER IN AN AGENCY

Definiteness in the terms of a contract between worker and agency insures an indispensable feeling of security on the part of both in regard to the social case worker's tenure in the agency. No contract, however, can reflect the full professional obligation of the agency to its staff. As we have already pointed out, the maintenance of high standards of social case work practice is dependent preeminently upon professional growth in the personnel of social case work. This professional growth is a natural by-product of the daily experience of the social case worker in the field. Daily experience in the field, however, needs to be supplemented by other professional experiences if anything like maximum professional development is to be achieved by social case workers. Many such experiences can be made possible for social case workers only with the co-operation of the agency.

Among the more obvious ones which are completely within the control of the agency and which will contribute directly to its efficiency are such opportunities as are afforded by individual projects for study with time allowed by the agency for the purpose, an equitable policy regarding promotion both in salary and responsibility, participation in study groups within the agency.

A privilege which is possible only with the cooperation of the agency is leave of absence for study, on some occasions with salary and even with the agency defraying, in addition, a part of the expense. Attendance at national and state conferences with some regularity is also indispensable to sound professional development. The sabbatical year has not yet become common in social case work, although it has been adopted to a limited extent. It is also due to the social case worker that he have the freest possible access to opportunities offering new positions in other agencies. Since one of the problems in social case work is to define ways of lengthening the tenure of social case workers as social case workers, the principle of staff development involved in these privileges should be recognized as part of agency policies.

PROFESSIONAL OBLIGATIONS OF THE CASE WORKER TO HIS ORGANIZATION

Since social case work is carried on almost exclusively through the medium of organizations, it is obvious that the standing of social case work agencies is the concern not merely of boards of directors but, in an equally vital sense, of members of the profession. It seems clear, therefore, that a contractual agreement between the social case worker and his agency can no more define the full obligation of the worker to the agency than it can define the full obligation of the agency to the worker. The most obvious obligation of a social case worker to his organization would seem to be to give the best that he has of professional skill to his work, and this should mean continuous effort by the social case worker to use every resource which is open to him professionally to increase his efficiency. In view of the almost universal overloading of social case workers by agencies, we hesitate to suggest that overtime is inevitable. Nevertheless it seems to be in practically every field of activity which is professional in character. The present excess of overtime in social case work could be materially reduced by an increase in the resources of agencies, which is primarily the responsibility of the board of directors, and it could be still further reduced by better organization of time and existing resources which is partly the responsibility of social case workers themselves.

A second obligation of the social case worker is that of loyalty to the policies and regulations of the organization. We believe and shall reiterate the belief later that the members of the staff of an agency for social case work should have an opportunity to participate in the formulation of policies. At times disagreement by the individual worker with the policies of his organization is inevitable. The staff of a social case work agency, however, represent a group which, with respect to many of its important activities, must act as a group. It must be assumed that policies once adopted by an agency are binding upon its entire personnel, including members of the board, members of the staff and members of the volunteer force. Good teamwork requires willingness to abide by group decisions. The social case worker who finds himself in revolt against the policy of his organization has only three courses open to him. He may restrain his tendency to revolt and abide by the decisions of the organization; he may do this and also exert his influence fairly within the organization for a change in policy; or he may resign. Any person who chooses to ally himself with a group sacrifices some measure of freedom. The physician in private practice, the artist, and the reformer may be as markedly individualistic as they choose to be. The contribution of the social case worker, however, to progressive social welfare can at the present time be made only through organizations and for many years to come there is not likely to be any considerable development of free-lance social case work. Under these circumstances, organization loyalty would seem to be a prime responsibility of the case worker, not merely in the interests of his agency but in his own interests as well, not to speak of those of the community at large.

Another question of organization loyalty arises when the work of the organization is judged in the community by the conduct of the staff. We believe that an organization has no right to concern itself with the private affairs of its employees, unless their private affairs reflect disadvantageously upon the organization. The pursuit of this argument leads quickly into areas where one can hardly tread surefootedly. Freedom of speech and other phases of individual liberty, one likes to think, are part of the bill of rights of mankind. No social worker loses all his rights as a citizen and an individual because he becomes part of an organization. Nevertheless, regardless of any philosophy of individual liberty, social case workers whose professional standing makes them assets to an organization inevitably represent that organization in many relationships outside the boundaries of their immediate professional duties. A social worker whose high professional attainments may be an asset to his organization may become a liability if, because of his personal conduct, he alienates from the organization a measure of the community's moral support which, in the interests of general social welfare, it ought not to lose.

Staff Relationships

In the preceding discussion of the contractual and ethical obligations of the agency in regard to the professional development of the social case worker we have suggested some of the staff relationships which would tend to promote the morale of a competent agency for social case work. We believe in general that the supervision of a staff should be conceived of as having two functions: first, to keep the work of the agency up to the standard it has set for itself; and second, to promote the professional development of the staff. Supervision which is based upon democratic organization of staff relationships will be more conducive to the development of morale than supervision which is autocratic in character. One of the most important implications in a democratic organization of staff relationships is that it will give the entire professional staff an opportunity to participate in formulating the policies of the agency. It is also indispensable to a democratic organization that there be sufficiently frequent conferences of the members of the staff to insure their vital participation in general discussions of the work of the agency.

A sound procedure of supervision will include methods of appraising the work of every member of the staff. It will also include such a routine of staff contacts as will give to the staff members the feeling of easy access to all the members of the supervisory force from the general executive down. Every social case worker is entitled also to a periodical survey of his work and progress in consultation with a supervisor. Moreover, recognition of achievement by social case workers should be given whenever the occasion arises. Such recognition is to a large extent indicated by promotion and increase in salary but it should not be left to be taken for granted. Few human beings fail to derive security and stimulus to sustained effort from appreciation on the part of those under whom they work. This is as true of supervisors in relationship to general executives and of general executives in relationship to boards of directors as it is of workers holding subordinate positions. Assuming it to be true, recognition by supervisors of achievement on the part of social case workers would seem to be an easy and telling method of contributing to staff morale. We should like to add that in our judgment the value of this practice is not in the least sentimental but wholly practical.

We realize that agencies for social case work vary greatly in size and resources. Some of the suggestions made in this chapter are obviously beyond the possibility of achievement in many agencies with high standards of competency. These suggestions, however, have rather more than the force of illustrations. We believe that none of them is wholly fanciful for every one is in effect somewhere in the social case work field. Moreover they are presented here more as indications of tendencies in the management of personnel than as forming collectively a comprehensive discussion of this problem. There are many aspects of personnel management, particularly in specific social case work which we have not covered. We have attempted to do no more than to suggest the spirit in which the problem should be approached by the administration of an agency and to present some concrete illustrations of ways in which particular agencies have infused this spirit into the mechanics of their personnel relationships.

PART IV

The Division of Labor Among Agencies for Social Case Work

Assuming Competent Agencies in the Various Case Work Fields, What Is a Desirable Basis for a Division of Labor in Social Case Work in a Local Community?

CHAPTER XVII

THE DIVISION OF LABOR IN HUMAN ACTIVITIES HAVING TO DO WITH THE TREATMENT OR DEVELOPMENT OF THE INDIVIDUAL

Social case work is one of many forms of professional service which have to do with the treatment or development of the individual. Among others may be included medicine, the administration of justice, the ministry and education. If one goes back far enough into human history, one may find most of these functions combined in the service of a single person or authority. The family patriarch may have exercised all of them, the church has certainly exercised most of them.

As these services developed into separate institutions, one finds the emergence of professions whose work at the outset seems not to overlap. The concern of medicine has been with the treatment of the sick, of the courts with the enforcement of the criminal law, of the ministry with the spiritual well-being of the individual, of the school with the imparting of knowledge to pupils, of social work (or its forerunners) with the relief of human need. It is not altogether fanciful to suggest an historical stage in the development of civilization which presents a complete division of labor among these fields of service. Points of contact they undoubtedly had, but of conscious overlappings there were probably few.

Within comparatively recent times, historically considered, each of these types of service discovered that its function was not exclusively to cure, to punish, to save, to teach or to succor mankind but that its service, like the others, must be made to contribute to the general state of well-being of those with whom it dealt. There is a time in the history of each of them, never chronologically definite, when it becomes aware of the whole man. The inevitable result is a widening of its sphere of interest. One finds medicine concerning itself with the intelligence, with the economic status and even with the spiritual state of its patients. One finds the court, originally perhaps in connection with its treatment of children, concerned with family relationships, economic problems, school attendance, health, intelligence and spiritual well-being. A modern school system has a department devoted to the testing of intelligence, to the physical examination of school children, to the industrial future of children, to the relationship between the school and home. This general trend is part of what is ordinarily spoken of as the socializing of human activities. An inevitable result of this development has been the overlapping of fields of service which, historically have been distinct.

The problem of the division of labor, therefore, is not peculiar to social case work. In a broad sense there is a community problem of the division of labor among these forms of service to the individual of which social case work is one. One phase of that problem is the inevitable assumption by each of these organized activities that its historical competence in its own field is adequate for these broader functions which a socialized conception of its task has revealed. We are not concerned with the relationships of other professional groups to each other. Our concern at this point is with the division of labor between social case work on the one hand and education, courts, medicine, the ministry, and so on, on the other. The basis for this division of labor at the present time lies in the recognition by these other fields of activity that social case work is a form of service which, for their own purposes, is an indispensable supplement to their own. The problem of the division of labor among the various professions regarded as necessary in the administration of education, of medicine, of the court, is probably not completely solved. In so far as social case work is concerned in that problem, the solution lies in the increasingly effective contribution of social case work as a supplementary service to these other fields of activity, a contribution which will carry its own demonstration of value.

The division of labor among social case work agencies as an assignment to this Committee is only indirectly concerned with this larger problem of the division of labor among several professional fields.

The assignment to this Committee relates to the division of labor among the various specific fields of social case work itself. Specializations in practice are not peculiar to social case work. They are found in practically all professions. They usually represent a concentration of interest upon some one phase of the whole professional field which, before specializations appeared, was assumed to be completely within the powers of each individual practitioner.

The reasons for the development of specialization are various. It is frequently compelled by the growth in knowledge which makes it impossible for one practitioner any longer to develop an adequate understanding of his whole field or an adequate mastery of the increasing measures for dealing with its problems. It is sometimes the result of the preference of individuals or groups to concentrate upon some part of the field which interests them more than others. It sometimes results from practical recognition of the fact that a problem is too big to be handled effectively by one person or group but must be split up into parts, although the several parts or many of them may make no essentially different demands upon the professional skill of those who concentrate upon them. All of these and other explanations of the trend towards specialization tend to justify it as a phase of the developing efficiency of professional service.

In social case work the problem of the division of labor has two phases: first, among different fields of social case work defined according to differences in the human needs they serve which demand different social case work skills; second, the division of labor between agencies in the same field of social case work but under different auspices in the same community, as for instance public and private agencies doing family case work. The problem of the latter would seem simple of solution. It is sometimes difficult, however, because of differences of standards among agencies working in the same field within the same territory and because frequently agencies working on what is essentially the same specific problem insist upon distinctions, justifying separate organizations and special terminology when those distinctions do not exist. Therefore, in our discussion later of some principles which should govern the division of labor, we have had both phases of the problem in mind.

CHAPTER XVIII

THE DEVELOPMENT OF THE DIVISION OF LABOR IN SOCIAL CASE WORK

The origin of social case work is not chronologically fixed. Historically one finds many traditional forms of service, such as the care of the poor, the treatment of the sick, provision for children, and so on, administered in a spirit of concern for the beneficiaries which puts them spiritually at least in line with modern social case work. While it does not seem possible or necessary to fix the emergence of the various forms of social case work now current, some historical developments are worth noting as having some bearing at least upon the development of a diversified agency equipment in the social case work field. Among these developments might be mentioned:

Rise of the English Poor Law.
Development of placing out work for children.
Establishment of the charity organization movement.
Establishment of the juvenile court and the probation system.
Development of parole and after-care for the insane and for prisoners.
Establishment of medical social work.
Development of visiting teaching.
Emergence of psychiatric social work.

Most of these developments have had a continuous history as definite movements up to the present time. Many of them made use from the beginning of certain principles of practice which still seem to be valid. Few of them, however, began with any highly developed conception of social case work as it is understood today. This conception, however, has grown directly out of the work of these historic movements with some contribution to its general body of knowledge and methods from all of them although the contribution of some came earlier than did that of the others.

In so far as the division of labor among social case work agencies is a problem whose solution presents difficulties, it is partly due to the origin and development of many of these movements as expressions of a philanthropic spirit rather than as programs based upon any deep analysis of the needs to be attacked or a consciousness of proved methods of service. Miss Addams has spoken of the beginnings of the settlement movement as representing the development of the sentiment of universal brotherhood from an emotion into a motive. The same statement could have been made about the beginnings of social case work. As, later, social case work through its own cumulative achievement developed from a motive into a function, it still remains true that the motive aspect has been a dominant factor in preserving the traditional sanctions for the types of organizations and the original definitions of field which came to the fore early in the history of social case work as philanthropy. Charity, alms giving, asylums, have been and continue to be characteristic of the socialized community. These, however, are not necessarily social case work. It is probably true that the division of labor in social case work is a problem partly because of a certain entrenched institutional pride, strongly reflecting the motive of service, but too little cognizant of the necessity in modern life of organizing service in terms of function. This factor probably operates more strongly among the agencies in a community operating in a given field (children's agencies, family agencies, hospitals, etc.) than among the different fields of social case work themselves.

In attempting to find a solution of the problem of the division of labor, one must be prepared to recognize, first, that the socializing of the various historic fields of human service dealing with human beings has broadened the scope of each of them to the point where its area overlaps those of other services; and, second, that some of the difficulties in the way of a sound division of labor are inherent in the traditional sentiment which has grown up around certain forms of social and charitable work and are deeply rooted in the motives of those who established them and those who have perpetuated them.

CHAPTER XIX

SOME PRINCIPLES GOVERNING THE DIVISION OF LABOR IN SOCIAL CASE WORK

In assigning to the Committee the question—"What is a desirable division of labor among the social case work agencies of an American community?" the Milford Conference instructed the Committee to assume "competent agencies." Making this assumption, the Committee suggests the following principles as essential to a sound division of labor among case work agencies:

A. *A social case work agency should do a complete social case work job with its cases and should transfer a case only when the services of another agency are clearly needed.* As will appear later (see Principle H) the Committee believes that co-operative treatment, that is to say, treatment involving simultaneous work by two or more agencies, is not only inevitable but highly desirable. We believe, moreover, that in a well organized community with competent agencies co-operative treatment will increase. Nevertheless, our first principle governing the division of labor is that the social case work agency, whatever its auspices, should do a complete case work job on its cases in its own field, and should transfer a case only when an adequate diagnosis shows that the services of another agency are needed. We believe that at the present time agencies frequently request other organizations to take over part of the responsibility for treatment which they should assume themselves. Part I of this report on "Generic Social Case Work" clearly indicates that every social case work agency should be prepared to do work as broad in scope, as precise in procedure, and as complete in the extension of its services as the demands of the individual case requires. In actual practice every agency should do work of this calibre with a substantial segment of its case load. This statement should be interpreted in connection with the discussion of Principles E and H.

B. *There should be no diagnostic authority without treatment responsibility and no treatment responsibility without diagnostic authority.* It has been the practice in some localities to ask one agency to base its treatment upon the investigation or the diagnosis of another agency. This has usually been accompanied by the assumption that the treatment agency was not free to make its own investigation and diagnosis.

We believe this practice to be bad for two reasons. In the first place, we believe that treatment loses the opportunity to be completely effective unless it is continuously in the hands of one agency from the time of application. Exceptions to this statement must, of course, be noted in cases where a transfer of responsibility from one agency to another is desirable.

In the second place, we believe that in the long run neither investigation nor diagnosis can be adequately or safely made except by an authority which is also responsible for treatment. We recognize the consulting diagnostician in professional practice when his service is co-ordinated with that of the authority having full treatment responsibility. The test of investigation and of diagnosis lies in the results of treatment. Those experts and those organizations which are not continuously subjected to the test which their own treatment affords for their own investigations and diagnoses are not likely to make investigations and diagnoses that are sound. Only experience in treatment can insure that investigation and diagnosis cover adequately the foundations essential to treatment. We believe, therefore, that it is indispensable to a competent agency that it make its own investigation and diagnoses.

C. *A transfer of a case from one organization to another should be made only when there is good reason to believe that better service will result from such transfer.* The word transfer has come to mean a changing of responsibility from one organization to another, based upon the findings of the organization of origin. We believe that there is a distinct loss of momentum in a transfer and therefore that the only justification for it is the prospect of more effectual service of the specific type which the second agency is able to give. We believe that a transfer is usually to be preferred to a refer, as between different fields of social case work, because it includes the responsibility both for further diagnosis and for treatment (see B).

Transfer from one specific social case work field to another may in certain instances be avoided by consultation between staff members of the organization in charge with staff members of the organization specially equipped to render service in view of new developments in the case, using the experience and the skill of the second agency, much as a physician or psychiatrist or psychiatric social worker may be used, so as to undertake treatment in the light of all the community's experience that is available.

D. *The larger the organization the more remote is its management from the needs which it serves.* The principle of the concentration of administrative auspices has gained considerable ground in modern life. Industrial combinations, mass production, large hospitals and the large university are illustrations. Even in industry, however, where the trend is especially strongly marked, there are leaders who believe that the very large administrative unit has disadvantages. Social agencies, as they grow in size and complexity, suffer not only the general difficulties attendant upon such growth, but also special disadvantages due to the nature of their work.

The combination of various social case work services in one agency and the development of large agencies in any one field of social case work may go so far as to be incompatible with the most effectual service to clients. A single executive cannot at the present time acquire the range of knowledge and experience essential to do justice to several fields of social case work.

An executive must be not only an executive, but he must also supply some measure of leadership in all of the activities of his organization. The scope of the organization's effective service therefore is determined in part by its leadership.

We believe that social work is a unified profession and not an aggregate of specialties. As we have repeatedly pointed out, this means that the generic aspects of social case work are more important in the equipment of the social case worker than its specific aspects. Administratively, however, all social work is specific. Experience clearly shows the difficulty of expanding the number of social case work functions carried by one agency without fostering some of them at the expense of others. This is largely because in these days of complex resources, diversified problems and rapidly expanding knowledge, the executive at the head of a big organization can hardly be equally a leader in several fields of work. Good social case work, moreover, demands that a high degree of freedom and initiative be given the social case worker, because factual material, philosophy and methods are in a rapidly evolving stage, and because social case work is a creative activity. From one point of view, therefore, the administration of a social case work agency is a problem in according to the staff of social case workers the largest degree of freedom and initiative consistent with desirable uniformity in the applications of the standards and policies of the organization. The mechanics indicated in this situation would seem to involve a minimum reliance on rules and regulations and a maximum reliance upon attitudes and practices which foster staff morale.

Yet in an organization employing a large personnel coherence and economy in the work of the staff make inevitable an extensive use of rules and regulations. Staff morale is fostered chiefly by close personal contact among the personnel of the organization with special emphasis upon personal contacts between management and staff. In an organization so large that these contacts become difficult, especially when they are difficult because of the inaccessibility of the executives, there may be a tendency to achieve desirable uniformity in agency practice by increasing recourse to rules and regulations with a minimum reliance upon staff morale. By and large, morale seems to be influenced by the size of the agency and it does provide a valid if somewhat indefinite test of wholesome growth in size.

Another administrative problem which grows more difficult with increase in size is the problem of measuring results. It would be reassuring to many persons deeply interested in social case work to be able to set up checks upon results as specific, as easily made and as convincing as are output, sales, earnings and costs in industry, but at the present time social case workers are only beginning to develop measurements for the results of social case work and are not likely ever to be able to establish checks upon efficiency as specific as those now used in industry. In the absence of such specific tests, the greatest resource of the executive in social case work is his ability to keep closely in touch with the routine work of his organization. Obviously the larger the organization the more difficult does this become.

A more positive argument for more, and therefore smaller, rather than fewer, and therefore larger, agencies, lies in the greater number of opportunities provided by a larger number of agencies for the service of laymen, as board members, in committee work, as volunteers, etc. The use of laymen is quite as practicable for the large organization as for the small, but the interest of laymen in volunteer service depends largely upon the degree of responsibility involved in the tasks they are asked to assume, and in so far as the most responsible tasks open to laymen are those having to do with participation in the making of programs and the leadership of the organization within the community, such opportunities would seem to decrease with the concentration of administrative auspices of social work.

To some extent all of the disadvantages of the large organization mentioned in the foregoing discussion may be offset by the decentralization of administration. In a large community the organization which adopts the district system and the state-wide organization which develops a high degree of local regional autonomy will find it possible to safeguard some of the essential administrative relationships which might otherwise be lost in the large organization.

E. *Social case work organized as a supplementary service within other programs (mural social case work) will be determined, as to scope and tenure on the cases treated, by the requirements of these other programs.* We have already suggested our belief that the social case work agency should do a complete social case work job with its own cases. We recognize, however, that work on cases in the hospital social service department, in the visiting teaching department, in the probation department, etc., must be terminated when the purposes of the organizations served by these departments have been fulfilled. We believe that the work of such departments should meet the full implications of our conception of generic social case work. The agencies which they serve, however, will frequently need to close their cases because their medical, legal, or educational jurisdiction ceases and ordinarily they should do so. In many cases thus terminated, there may remain a vital need for continuing social case work service. In such cases both sound division of labor and ethical considerations demand that they be transferred to other agencies whose tenure of service is not thus limited.

F. *A community's social equipment should include social case work under both public and private auspices.* We believe that this proposition is almost axiomatic. There is, however, in this country, a sufficiently strong remnant of belief that social case work under public auspices must necessarily be so inefficient as to be discouraged whenever possible. In so far as the report of this Committee can contribute to the elimination of this remnant of tradition we should like to do so.

For example, during the last decades of the nineteenth century particularly, it was strongly urged that public outdoor relief should be abolished. This crusade represented a revolt against a type of public administration in the field of relief which was not only inefficient and wasteful but was, in the judgment of workers in charitable agencies, a downright menace to family life. It is probably true that one result of distrust of public outdoor relief was an increase in the breaking up of families and in the use of institutions for the care of children. At the present time, there undoubtedly is both in public agencies and in private agencies every problem of efficiency which was current fifty years ago, but we realize that these problems cannot be solved by complete separation of the interests of public and private agencies. When one surveys the field of social case work comprehensively it becomes clear that whatever be the inherent limitations either of public administration or of the private agency, both are essential to complete community service to those members of the community whose capacities to organize their own normal social activities are impaired.

At the present time the argument regarding both public and private activity in the field of social welfare as essential in community equipment does not rest solely upon the conviction that the older distrust of public administration was ill-founded. There are many arguments on the positive side. It is clear that neither governmental agencies nor private societies can ever alone carry the social case work burden of the community. Moreover, within the last twenty-five years there has been ample evidence of efficient administration of social case work under public auspices and we believe that the present trend in the field of governmental social case work is in the direction of increased efficiency and a wider diffusion of high standards. There is no form of social case work which is not now being undertaken and efficiently administered somewhere in this country by governmental agencies.

A still more cogent reason for emphasizing the need of social case work under public auspices lies in the fact that some problems of social case work can be more effectively handled under public auspices than they can ever be by private agencies. This is largely true of cases in which legal authority behind the treatment efforts of the social case worker is either advantageous or indispensable.

The logical division between public and private effort has not yet been defined with precision. Experience, however, seems to indicate the soundness of certain tendencies. It is clear to the Committee that what we have said in Principle A in this chapter applies with as much force to a public agency as to a private agency: a social case work agency should do a complete social case work job with its cases. This means that the public agency should do adequately that which it undertakes to do and this proposition raises at once the question of the practice which is not uncommon in American communities of supplementing through private resources the work of the public department. We believe that the supplementing of the programs of public departments by money or service secured from private agencies is justifiable only as a demonstration, a part of a co-operative effort, involving both agencies, to develop for the public department sufficient money and equipment to enable it to do its full task. The supplementing of public social case work by private agencies if continued too long may easily prevent the development of adequate standards in public work.

It is probably true that a private agency which is free from the rigid limitations of scope sometimes imposed by legislation upon the public agency may show a greater flexibility in the use of its resources to meet the changing needs of the community. To the extent that this is true a division of labor between the two in any community would in general reserve for the private agency those community needs for which such flexibility is required. It has also been recognized that the private agency may experiment and conduct demonstrations with reference to new types of effort to an extent that would hardly be suitable for a public agency.

Other suggestions for the division of labor between public and private agencies would undoubtedly be found in the current practice of many American communities. The Committee has not had time to assemble information regarding such situations. It includes here, however, two formulations on this subject. One of these was prepared by C. C. Carstens, Chairman of the Committee on Children for the National Conference of Social Work in 1915. The other was drafted by a committee of the American Association for Organizing Family Social Work after considerable study of the subject.

FUNDAMENTAL PRINCIPLES IN DIVISION OF LABOR BETWEEN PUBLIC AND PRIVATE AGENCIES DOING WORK WITH CHILDREN[1]

1. The Federal Children's Bureau is the most recent development of the nation's interest in work for children. Investigation, publicity and community education seem to have been its work up to this time, although there is a clearly marked tendency to enlarge the scope of the federal powers.
2. The state is the most useful area for the development of standards and machinery in the care of children of whatever type. The county as an administrative subdivision of the state becomes an indispensable unit of service in most parts of the country. In certain New England states the town or a union of towns and, in certain sparsely populated states, a union of counties may serve this purpose.
3. Subject to the limitations which the federal and state constitutions have for the time being established, there is no task which the community in its public capacity may not undertake and under certain circumstances should not undertake. The trend of social thought is clearly in the direction of broadening the interests and activities of the community in its public capacity. There are still those who would go slow in helping on such a development, but there are only a few who will now deny the public the right to undertake all forms of child helping work when it is done ineffectively or not at all from private resources.
4. For the near future public boards or departments should devote themselves to such children's work as is based on principles that are well established, require the more permanent care, are more general in their application or contain an element of compulsion or control, while private organizations should seek development in directions that are more experimental, require more temporary care, are most unusual in their application or are carried on with the co-operation of the families benefited.
5. The division of responsibility in the care of children caused by the granting of public subsidies to private charity or by adding public officials to private boards of trustees,

---

[1]From the Proceedings of the National Conference of Social Work, Section on Children, 1915.

is against good public policy. Of all the principles that this report is undertaking to state, this one is likely to arouse the most controversy, for theory and practice are in this particular the farthest apart, but while there are sometimes compelling reasons for entering into a plan of public subsidies to private charities or for continuing it under certain circumstances, this is rarely done without embarrassments to both public and private interests.

6. When a private organization has clearly demonstrated the value of an experiment, it is in the community's interest that such a service in order that it may have a wider application or be rendered in a larger area, be extended to the state as soon as it is in position to equip itself for such service. All too frequently private societies are still standing in the way of the public's development by seeking to hold on to what as a rule can have only a limited application while under private direction. It is one of the important functions of a private society from time to time to see what functions that it has been undertaking may to advantage be transferred to the state as a whole, in order that the service may be broadened. For the proper development of such work, it may even then be wise that public and private bodies should for a period of time carry on the same or similar tasks side by side.

7. No public or private department in children's work is well equipped without a staff of social investigators and medical and mental experts who have the special education and training for their tasks at least equivalent to the equipment that a school system requires for its work. Such a staff must in addition be under the supervision of an experienced social work executive.

SUGGESTED DIVISION BETWEEN PUBLIC AND PRIVATE AGENCIES DOING FAMILY CASE WORK WHEN BOTH AGENCIES DO GOOD CASE WORK[1]

The Committee would submit the following conclusions (where both agencies are equipped to do good case work) :

1. That, ordinarily, both public and private agencies for family social work are needed and that they should be entirely distinct and independent of each other, with good team work between them. Either alone is unable to bear the full burden of need and insure progress.

   (a) The public agency alone is unstable and inclined to deteriorate.

   (b) The private agency alone cannot, ordinarily, limit its intake and do the intensive experimental work which is a very important contribution which only the private agency can make.

   (c) Combination plans of any type, whether of money or of personnel, tend to be unstable and to slow down the dvelopment of each agency. In some communities some combination plan may be a practical necessity, but the dangers and disadvantages involved need always be kept in mind.

2. With the two agencies working separately, division of work must depend upon the quality of work possible in each.

   (a) Where the public agency is not prepared to do social case work, we believe that no definite division should be attempted on type of case unless it is to leave to the public department the cases of old age and other permanent physical disability. With such a public agency, we believe that the two will very often have to supplement each other's work. The use of the social service exchange, and conference on cases will be necessary for satisfactory results. Any policy of supplementing one another's work on the same cases should however, always be regarded as temporary, and every effort should be made to induce the public agency to develop social case work.

   (b) Where there is some attempted social case work in the public department but of very much lower standard than that in the private agency, we believe there will need to be an effort to have each agency handle as fully as possible those cases which it undertakes, but that the division of work will need to be determined rather by conference on cases or by priority of entrance into the case than on the type of case.

   (c) When both agencies do good social case work, the Committee would suggest the following division:

   (1) That division of work be made on the basis of type of case.

   (2) That each agency should handle completely those cases for which it is responsible, except as joint plans may be undertaken in an occasional

---

[1]From a Report of the Committee on Relations with Public Departments of the American Association for Organizing Family Social Work, 1925. For full report address: Family Welfare Association of America, 130 East 22nd Street, New York City. (Price 10 cents.)

case by special conference. As transfer of cases from one agency to the other is undesirable if avoidable, the case should, so far as possible, be referred at its inception to the agency that will handle it.

(3) That the public agency should bear from the tax fund the heaviest part of the relief burden. To this end it may in general well take those cases in which the capacity for self-support does not exist in any considerable measure in the client himself and will not for a long time. This would include cases of old age, widows with young children, tuberculosis and other long continued disabilities.

This does not mean, however, that families needing more than temporary help should be turned over to the public department, nor that the public department should take only relief cases. In our opinion, the elements both of time and relief have been erroneously emphasized. Social case work is a process of developing personality. Personality must ordinarily be developed by slow processes of re-education and adjustment. And during that process, considerable relief may be needed over long periods of time. The private agency doing good social case work must therefore be prepared to handle long time problems involving relief.

(4) That the private agency should take cases that primarily involve personality problems calling for especially intensive work, which may or may not extend over a long period; and

(5) Cases involving experimental treatment (4 and 5 will frequently be identical).

(6) First applications of young, normally constituted families should go to the private society in the hope that timely and intensive case work may prevent demoralization and establish sound principles of family life.

(7) Cases potentially involving the need of social control—such as cases of mental trouble or of marital trouble—may well be the subject of careful conference between the two agencies as to which is in the best position to handle such cases. Probably in the less hopeless forms these are two types which peculiarly need intensive, long continued, personal service and experimental treatment. Whichever agency is in the best position to give such treatment should handle the case. The suggestion in Sections 4 and 5 above would indicate that that is likely to be the private agency.

G. *Relief work should be administered by the case work agency having responsibility for treatment.* We believe that the administration of relief is indispensable in good social treatment. The necessity for relief arises more frequently in some forms of social case work than in others, and it is an entirely legitimate form of co-operative treatment to leave those phases of treatment primarily concerned with relief to one agency and other phases to another. No agency, however, should undertake, or be expected to give, relief except when it has also at least partial diagnostic and treatment responsibility.

It is obvious that relief takes different forms. It may be free medical service; it may be the payment of board for a child temporarily away from its home; it may be a subsidy called a scholarship for school attendance; it may be a grant of money to cover the most necessary items in a family budget. Some forms of relief are more common in one field of work than another. In terms of the psychology of the client some forms of relief present different treatment problems than others. Our conception of generic social case work includes wise and effective administration of relief by every social case work agency.

We recognize that relief on the allowance plan to families in their own homes is predominantly the responsibility of the family field. The number of cases in which weekly family allowances should be given by other agencies because they present no need for treatment service from a family agency would be relatively small.

We recognize that relief-giving creates treatment problems of its own and we are aware of the aversion on the part of many forms of social case work to the development of their own relief funds.   Nevertheless, we believe that in so far as this is a problem of division of labor, each social case work agency should be prepared to administer relief in cases under treatment, except where it seems desirable to transfer to another agency not only the responsibility for relief, but also a definite responsibility for at least part of the treatment.

H. *Co-operative treatment involving on a single case the simultaneous work of two or more agencies is not only a normal aspect of the division of labor, but may be expected to increase.* The problems created by co-operative treatment may be solved in part by working agreements among social case work agencies which define in advance so far as may be possible, the types of cases which each will undertake to provide for.

It is to be expected, however, that there will constantly arise cases where the line of responsibility is not clear. We must expect honest differences of opinion in such matters, but we believe that these borderline cases can be effectively handled if their appearance is regarded as a normal feature of the social case work of the community. The obvious procedure for determining the respective responsibilities of agencies in such cases is conference between the representatives of the agencies concerned. We believe that such conferences should be undertaken with two important assumptions in mind: first, that an agreement as to the proper auspices for the handling of the case *must* be reached; and second, that in the interest of a progressive development of the division of labor in the community, a record of such agreements should be kept and periodically studied for whatever light they may throw upon the possible modification of existing working arrangements among agencies.

We suggest that the experience of agencies in such conferences should be an important source of data regarding the division of labor. They should, therefore, be handled in an entirely objective spirit, and we realize that they are being so handled in a great many communities at the present time. As a matter of record we suggest that the personnel of such conferences for a discussion of borderline cases might include successively the following groups:

1. A single case worker from each agency concerned.
2. Staff case workers plus supervisors from each agency concerned.
3. Staff case workers, supervisors, and executives from each agency concerned.
4. Staff members and board members from each agency concerned.
5. Representatives of each agency concerned with representatives of some general community agency, such as a council of social agencies.

As a practical aspect of co-operative treatment, we suggest that from the point where the second agency is drawn into a case and co-operative treatment begins, and continuously thereafter, there should be joint planning by the agencies concerned.

If it be recognized that borderline cases, where the division of responsibility is not clear, are inevitable and therefore entirely normal in the experience of a community, it should be possible to conduct such conferences in the spirit of experiment and group planning. The very existence of these borderline cases indicates a joint responsibility and therefore suggests a much greater community interest than lies in cases which are the responsibility of one agency exclusively. At no point in the work of an agency for social case work does it become so necessary to revise constantly its conception of its own community responsibilities as at the point where it undertakes, or where it or other agencies believe it should undertake, co-operative treatment.

PART V

Training for Social Case Work

CHAPTER XX

The Organization of Training at the Present Time

This Committee's original assignment on the subject of training was stated as follows: "to work out in addition to its other duties some plan of study of the various training activities in the social case work field along the lines which have been outlined." The Committee has not been able to make any special efforts to secure information regarding existing training activities and has been able to use in its discussions only such information regarding them as was already in the possession of its members. Furthermore, it has somewhat modified the original interpretation of this part of its assignment and presents in this part of the report its analysis of the training problem as it presents itself to agencies for social case work.

This problem may be stated as follows:

1. There is at the present time a lack of adequately trained personnel for social case work.
2. Since the schools of social work are not able to meet the demand the agencies are forced to undertake staff training on an apprentice basis.
3. Extension and institute courses chiefly for the further development of experienced workers are in growing demand.
4. Both schools and apprentice programs show wide diversity in educational standards and in the content of training offered.
5. There is a really serious lack of facilities for carrying on professional training, including teachers, teaching material and generally accepted standards regarding the content of the curriculum and methods of instruction.

The Objectives of a Training Program for Social Case Workers

The two leading objects of a training program for social case workers may be stated as follows:

1. To provide the student with an opportunity to acquire a thorough mastery of the subject matter of social case work as outlined in the preceding sections of this report which may be recapitulated under the following headings used as chapter headings in Parts II, III and IV:

Generic Social Case Work

    Deviations
    Norms
    Particularization of the Individual
    Methods
    Community Resources for Social Case Work
    Adaptation of Science and Experience
    Philosophy
    Social Treatment

A Competent Agency for Social Case Work
  Standards of Social Case Work
  Study of Social Case Work
  Organization
  Community Relationships
  Personnel

The Division of Labor Among Agencies for Social Case Work
  Division of Labor Among Professional Fields which Deal with the Individual
  The Development of Division of Labor in Social Case Work
  Some Principles Governing the Division of Labor in Social Case Work

2. To provide the student with opportunity to develop proficiency in the use of this subject matter through practice in doing social case work.

THE CURRICULUM

The curriculum of professional education for social case work whether in a professional school or in an apprentice agency may be divided into four parts:

1. The fundamental techniques of social work.
2. Adaptations of science and the experience of other fields of activity for the purposes of social work.
3. The practice of social case work.
4. The orientation of the social worker.

1. *The fundamental techniques of social work.* The fundamental techniques of social work are now generally recognized as social ease work, community organization, group work, social research, and, since social work is almost invariably carried on through the medium of organizations, we may add the technique of administration.

In practice the social case worker makes greater use of the technique of social case work than of the others. Both because they are indispensable to good social case work and because his later practice as a social case worker affords him limited opportunity to acquire them, these other techniques should be included in his training. All of these techniques are indispensable to the standard of social case work implied throughout this report.

The fundamental techniques of social case work are suggested in this report chiefly in the discussions of Particularization and Method in Part II. We cannot within the space of this report set up detailed syllabi for the subject matter of a curriculum. We indicate later in this chapter what seems to us the range of training experiences through which training in the different phases of social case work may be given. Whether training in the fundamental techniques of social case work be given in planned and supervised field experience or through courses, it should cover all of the detailed aspects of technique suggested by the chapter on Methods (see page 23).

The importance for the social case worker of the other fundamental techniques of social work is indicated in this report chiefly in the discussions of the competent agency, especially the chapters on The Study of Social

Case Work, Organization and Community Relationships and Responsibilities. Specific training in these techniques is essential to efficient practice of social case work.

2. *Adaptations of science and experience from other fields for the purposes of social case work.* In Chapter IX of Part II we have indicated the importance of these adaptations and have suggested that their content as the social case worker makes use of them has not been adequately formulated. That social case workers rely upon them in practice, however, is indicated by the appearance in Conference programs, training school curricula and social case work literature of such subjects as Industrial Problems, Mental Hygiene, The Immigrant, Health and Disease, The Standard of Living, The Living Wage, Child Psychology, Personality Problems, The Social Worker and The Law, etc.

At the present time the social case worker's grasp of this adapted subject matter is secured chiefly through analysis of his own experiences and through deliberate study of the subject matter in courses and reading. For the most part discussions of this subject matter either in courses or in books have been presented by authorities who are not social workers. Such discussions, even when an attempt is made to direct them towards the needs of social workers are not likely to be adequate for the purposes of social case work. Until social case workers have made progress with the comprehensive problem of research towards which the whole of this report points they will have to take advantage of such facilities as there are, and the experience of individual social workers and of the schools has demonstrated that it is possible with those facilities to organize training in this aspect of social case work. Its scope and details in any one training plan will depend upon the facilities available in the local community, but some measuse of it should be included in every training program.

3. *The practice of social case work.* The two parts of a curriculum already discussed are concerned primarily with the subject matter of generic social case work. The Practice of Social Case Work as a division of the curriculum covers both the subject matter of the specific field and field work, or that part of the curriculum which provides opportunity for the student to use, under supervision, what he has learned elsewhere. This may seem to overlap somewhat the previously discussed division of the Fundamental Techniques, but we believe that they should be considered separately and, where resources and time permit as they should in a school, that they should be taught separately.

The distinction between courses and planned and supervised field experience as methods of training in the fundamental techniques of social case work (generic social case work as the Committee uses that term) presents little difficulty. Both courses and field experience seem to us essential in a training program, and we do not regard the courses as exclusively theoretical and the field work as exclusively practical. Each should have, but in different degrees, both aspects.   In training at its best all of the aspects of the fundamental techniques of social case work are covered in both.   In so far as such items in these techniques as planning, diagnosis, etc., involve analysis and study, sound methods of class instruction will give to courses in these topics a distinct practical value.

The distinction between The Fundamental Technique of Social Case Work and The Practice of Social Case Work as divisions within a curriculum is less clear.   It will be recalled that this Committee believes the peculiar and distinctive aspects of each specific field of social case work to be largely an intensive development for its peculiar and distinctive purposes of some of the subject matter of generic social case work.   In other words family welfare, child welfare, medical social work, and so on, are largely adaptations and to a lesser degree supplementations of generic social case work.   Hence courses and field experience in these phases of social case work must inevitably provide some training in generic social case work.   We do not believe, however, either that single courses or experience in a single field can be adequate both for training in generic social case work and for training in specific social case work.   We suggest therefore that the trend in training should be towards the development of courses in the methods which are common to all fields of social case work divorced from their specific application in any one field and towards training programs which include field experience in more than one field.

The second and equally important reason for these two divisions in the curriculum is that courses in specific subject matter (family welfare, child welfare, etc.) should be more than courses in technique.   They should be courses in the adaptation of all the phases of social work described in this report, especially under generic social case work and the competent agency, to the requirements of the specific field.   They will therefore include deviations, history, philosophy and studies of facts as well as techniques.

4.   *The Orientation of the Social Worker.*   The subject matter of social case work is now so substantial that it must be analyzed into its elements, in order to be understood.   Whereas, for example, the term investigation, itself one of the elements of social case work, at one time almost suggested its own content, the nature and significance of investigation in social case work today cannot be understood without analyzing it into such aspects as social case history, interviewing, observation, and so on.   A training program therefore must be largely constructed of units which, while complete in themselves and therefore susceptible to treatment in separate discussions or courses, are nevertheless conceived as fractional parts of social case work.   The same is true in a sense of field experience.

This analysis of social case work into its elements for study and training has the effect of bewildering newcomers to the profession.   They seem to be engaged in taking apart something which it may be difficult if not impossible to get together again.   Most of the recruits to social case work have entered the field because as a field it made an appeal to them. The seemingly unrelated courses in isolated subjects which together make up a curriculum or the seemingly unrelated tasks which make up the routine of their field experiences in an agency may appear to have little logical connection. To the student it may look as though social case work had refined itself so far that the forest is not visible because of the trees.

Some such impression is inevitable if students are left with training experiences which are organized solely around the details of social case work. For this reason every curriculum should include somewhere the opportunity for the student to see social case work as a whole and its major emphases related to each other. This is partly the function of the discussion of the philosophy of social case work and it is partly the function of interpretation by the instructor of the student's training experiences and impressions. There is no better place to contribute to the orientation of the social case worker in training than in the supervision of his field work. When resources permit it can be effectively done also through courses which are philosophical and interpretive in character.

EXPERIENCES WHICH PROVIDE TRAINING

A training program is something more than an organization of subject matter. It must provide certain distinct training experiences through which familiarity with the subject matter and its use is acquired. Among these training experiences which must be specifically planned for are the following:

Planned and supervised experience in social case work.
The study of social case records.
Reading.
Attendance at courses.
Individual supervisory contacts.
Formulation of material under direction.
Observation.
Discussion.
Analysis, under supervision, of the student's own professional experience.

Each of the aspects of social case work which constitutes the subject matter of a chapter in Parts II, III or IV of this report can be included in a training program through one of these training experiences or a combination of them. Some of these training experiences lend themselves more effectively to certain aspects of the subject matter than do others.

Two of the aspects of social case work treated in separate chapters of this report, namely Organization and the Management of Personnel, present peculiar difficulties when the effort is made to incorporate them into a training program. Training in organization (Chapter XIV), is difficult because actual experience in organizing must ordinarily come rather late in the student's training, and because responsibility for executive work requires a considerable degree of maturity and seasoning. Students are frequently not ready for this particular experience on an adequate scale until after the present formal period of training is over (about two years). It should be possible, however, to introduce students, even in a brief training period, to important aspects of organization. Through familiarity with reports, through emphasis on the significance of working in an agency and through familiarity with office routine a foundation can be laid even within the training period for the development of executive ability. We should like, also, to recognize that at the present time it frequently seems necessary to select executives for social case work agencies from other fields of work in order to secure persons of proven executive capacity. Such persons, however proven they may be as executives, should as a part of their introduction to social case work have some opportunity to secure experience in the practice of this particular field.

The handling of personnel is a phase of administration. Training directed toward the development of proficiency in the task is difficult because, like training in organization, it presupposes students of considerable maturity and seasoning in the field. Nevertheless, certain types of training experience, undertaken for other immediate purposes, may be so handled as to develop in the student an awareness at least of the problems of personnel management. Such training experiences would include supervisory contacts, reading, courses and analysis of the student's own experiences in relationship to the organization and its personnel.

Some Implications of This Training

The foregoing list of training experiences reflects methods now in use for the training of social case workers. Each of them is familiar to everyone who has assumed responsibility for training either in a school or in an agency offering an apprentice program. While there is undoubtedly complete agreement among those responsible for training regarding the validity of these experiences, the pedagogical methods through which they are applied in different training schemes vary widely. Nothing like uniformity in pedagogical methods is either achievable or desirable. Nevertheless, we believe that the construction of sound educational standards and their general acceptance implies a greater approach to uniformity in pedagogy than now exists. Before such an approach can be effected, considerable research and exchange of experiences by trainers will be necessary. The Committee ventures to suggest, however, some pedagogical implications, in connection with some of these training methods, which suggest the beginnings of sound educational methods in the training of social case workers. We present the following analysis of the pedagogy underlying a few of these training experiences as suggestive only:

Planned and Supervised Experience. We have designated this method of training as "Planned and Supervised Experience" rather than as "Experience" because we are not discussing the professional development of the social case worker in general but that type of professional development which is achieved within a training scheme. Efficient social case workers were developed before any deliberate training schemes were organized. Human proficiency in any field of activity may owe more to the experience of the individual unaided by guidance, advice and interpretation from others than it does to any organized schemes of training. We are, however, discussing training programs. We, therefore, distinguish between experiences acquired by the individual on his own and experiences deliberately arranged as part of a training scheme. An agency of whatever type which offers the novitiate no more than an opportunity to gain experience may be offering him something valuable but it is not offering him training. If experience in doing social case work is to justify itself as part of an educational program, it must be planned and supervised.

From this it follows that the primary consideration in the supervision of students gaining experience in social case work must be the educational value of such experience to the student and not the administrative necessities of the agency.

In the organization and planning of experiences for training purposes stress should be laid upon the desirability of the repetition of a particular experience to whatever extent may be necessary to enable a student to grasp its significance. An ordered sequence in experiences from the less complicated to the more complicated is desirable with provision through supervision for making clear the relationship between them. Diversity in experience is also indispensable. In so far as time permits, the student's training period should provide him with some contact through social case work with the whole range of conceptions, facts and methods which make up the subject matter of generic social case work as well as with the specific aspects which characterize the specific field in which he is training. No function of supervision as a part of training experience is more important than its provision of the kind of leadership and interpretation which enables the student to see the essential unity in diversified experiences. On the other hand, from the point of view of breadth of conception and balance in the sense of values, it is probably desirable to give the student experiences under more than one supervisor and in more than one district or locality.

Supervisory Contacts. In planning the individual contact between the supervisor and the student emphasis should again be placed upon the paramount importance of making this contact educational for the student rather than making it serve the administrative necessities of the organization. It is recognized that the training opportunities offered by a social case work agency whether as part of an apprentice training scheme or as part of the field work program of a school of social work, must always be influenced by the administrative requirements of the agency. We may go further and assert that in the long run professional education is most effective when that part of it which is acquired through practice has been secured in an agency functioning normally as part of the community's social equipment rather than in a specially set up laboratory for social case work.   Nevertheless, since we are discussing training and not sheer experience, we insist that the supervision of the student in a training program is primarily for the purpose of contributing to the education of the student as a social case worker and not for the purpose of making the student of maximum immediate value to the agency. These two things may amount in practice to much the same thing but a training program as a training program will, in the long run, be more effective if it is dominated by the first point of view rather than the second.

Supervisory contacts may be provided for students in groups but the routine of supervision must include ample opportunity for individual conferences between supervisor and student.   They should be frequent enough to enable the supervisor to keep in touch with the progress of the student and to prevent him from floundering and to give the student the feel of having access to the supervisor when he needs him.   It is probably not desirable to follow a fixed schedule of contacts with the individual student and apparently no definite rule can be set up as to the frequency with which such conferences should be held.   We believe, however, that in any training scheme they should be not less often than once a week.

The handling of such conferences with students calls for teaching skill We believe that students develop more rapidly, more confidently and more substantially when they have no sense of being under the thumb of a supervisor but are rather allowed a reasonable degree of initiative.   Supervision is most educational when it abandons the method of prescribing what students should do and criticizing their work according to their success or failure in meeting the prescriptions of the supervisor and substitutes the method of encouraging the students to do their own thinking and planning, so far as is permissible with safety to the work of the organization, and makes it possible for them to progress by analyzing their own results in conference with the supervisor.

Projects for Study.   The study project as a pedagogical method is useful for the development of a student's analytical faculty and capacity for original thinking.   Projects give useful practice in the anaylsis of a student's own experience, in the use of established methods and in the preparation of material for presentation to audiences and in print.   Many of the training schools and many of the agencies which conduct apprentice training programs make use of study projects.   Even simple projects may be so supervised as to give students an understanding of the implications of research and of the differences between scientific study and the preparation of propagandist material. Agencies which, as apprentice training centers or as field work stations for schools of social work, are responsible for student training, find it possible to relate study projects by students to the kind of responsibility for the study of social case work which is suggested in Chapter XIII, of this report, as one of the responsibilities of a competent social case work agency. The following are illustrations of study projects of this sort which are found to be within the range of students:

Study of attempts to provide individualized recreation programs for the members of three families under treatment.

A study of the interplay of several agencies as revealed by the case history of one family.

A study of industrial readjustment in eleven cases of handicapped men.

Reading. Reading is a means of opening up a wide range of accumulated experience which is not available in any other form. Continuous contact with literature which bears on the field is indispensable to the professional development of the social case worker. Therefore, it is important that a student during his training should both develop the habit of reading and become familiar with such literature. It is more valuable for the student to select his reading upon a particular problem from a variety of sources, if available, than to confine himself to one book or one author.

Reading as an assignment in a training program may serve as a medium for the further development of the subject matter of social case work in training programs whose allotment of time is limited. It is even more important in an apprentice training plan as a means of introducing the student to aspects of the subject matter for which no other training experiences are available. A good library of social work (and every social case worker should have access to one) will provide reading along both lines.

Courses. Any of the topics covered by this report would lend itself to treatment in a course. Some of them for the purposes of training can be handled more effectively in courses than otherwise. Among these would be such topics as:

History of social work.
Norms.
Adaptations of science to the requirements of the social worker.
Philosophy.
Organization.
Publicity.
Any phase of the practice of social case work for which no good field experience is available.

It is suggested that apprentice programs should make the fullest possible use of existing courses rather than to attempt to organize courses within the agency when others in the same subject matter are already available in the community. Provision should be made within the apprentice program for the correlation of such courses with the field work of the student.

In organization of courses case material adapted for teaching purposes is essential. There is a growing preference for other methods of course instruction than the lecture or textbook method, especially for the case method which permits the discussion of philosophical, theoretical and factual subject matter as implications of concrete situations.

Discussion. In listing discussion as a pedagogical method, the Committee has in mind nothing narrow or technical. We merely wish to emphasize the fact that professional growth is largely a matter of discussion of professional problems with other persons. Discussion is an important part of any good course in social case work and an important part of supervisory contacts. Construing the term "discussion" broadly for training purposes, we suggest that an important part of the training of the social case worker is an opportunity to see experts engaged in discussing the same kind of problems which he is being trained to handle. This means attendance by the student at case conferences, staff meetings and other group conferences. The participation of the student in such conferences may include, also, practice in the presentation of material and presiding over discussions. A certain facility in the organization of one's facts is essential to success even in unorganized casual discussion with other individuals. This leads us to suggest the value in a training scheme of frequent opportunities for students to discuss among themselves in wholly informal and unorganized fashion problems arising in their training experiences.

Some Minimum Standards for Training at the Present Time

We suggest the following as representing the minimum standards which should be set for the organization of training at the present time:

A. Apprentice Training

1. It must be conceived of as training and not as mere experience.
2. Apprentice training should be conceived as a course extending over a fixed period. The length of the period should be determined by the proportion of time allotted weekly for definite training experiences.
3. It must, so far as possible, make use of all the types of training experience discussed in this section of the Report, but will naturally place greatest reliance upon planned experience and supervisory contacts. Its more limited use of such methods as "courses," "reading" and "study projects" implies a great responsibility upon apprentice supervisors for broad and penetrating interpretation to students of their practical experiences.
4. As a minimum of time for training outside of actual practice in social case work, we suggest twelve hours a week, of which four hours should be devoted to class work and eight hours to reading, study projects, reports, and so on, related to the class work. Twelve hours a week we interpret to be approximately the equivalent of one and a half days. The student should be free for at least this much time during the working hours of the week for class work and assignments in connection with it, although we recognize that a reasonable measure of overtime may be expected from apprentice workers.

5. The time allotted to class work should not be interrupted by the case work demands of the agency except in distinct crises or emergencies.
6. Since the time available for courses and classes in an apprentice program is limited, the courses organized should be in subject matter designed to round out the training of the student rather than in subjects with which familiarity can be gained through planned experience.
7. Apprentice training should provide ample opportunity for participation by the student in staff conferences, committee work, and so on.
8. The reading prescribed for apprentice workers should not be restricted to the subject matter of the courses offered but should include reading in those aspects of social work with which the apprentice training facilities do not provide other points of contact.
9. As a final minimum condition of apprentice training, we repeat that an apprentice training scheme should be dominated by the educational needs of the student and not by the administrative necessities of the agency.

B. School Training

1. It should provide a course of training covering two academic years.
2. Its curriculum should be founded upon opportunities for field work and we believe that approximately one-half of the time represented in the two-year period should be spent in supervised field work. We suggest this fundamental importance of practice as a part of the professional curriculum because we believe that all professional education finds its chief educational focus in the use by the student of what he is learning.
3. The courses offered by the school should be so organized as to cover all of the main aspects of social case work as indicated in this Report.
4. The class time of the students should be interruptable when the field work assignments of the students are sufficiently critical and emergent to demand immediate attention.
5. An internship year, following the two-year curriculum in the school itself, is desirable before the award of the school diploma.
6. Courses in the fundamental techniques of social case work and in the practice of social case work (see pages 78-79) should be given by instructors whose qualifications are at least those for senior membership in the American Association of Social Workers.
7. It should admit as students only college graduates or those with equivalent preparation and should further select students on the basis of their intellectual and temperamental qualifications for social work.

CHAPTER XXI

The Future Development of Training for Social Case Work

Any attempt to formulate the desirable future of professional education for social case work must be based upon recognition of the following needs which such education must serve:

Agencies need qualified personnel.

Individual social case workers need professional development for which opportunities for periodical contact with professional education are essential.

The profession of social work needs the stability which other professions have developed, partly through well-established programs of professional education.

Beginning at the present and looking forward to a future in which professional education for social work tends towards the complete meeting of these needs, we find that the facilities required in this development at the present time, and probably for a long time to come, must include apprentice programs, schools of social work, and opportunist facilities, particularly for practicing case workers, of the "extension" and "institute" type.

In any community where there is a school of social work we believe that it is better for the agency to correlate its scheme of training with the school rather than to set up a plan of training of its own. We believe strongly that in the long run the most desirable form of training is school training.

A social case work agency must maintain a standard of work which implies a staff whose qualifications are attained in part by experience. Therefore, every social case work agency has responsibility in terms of training of its staff; if school graduates are not available for vacancies and school facilities not available for the training of new members of its staff, then the agency has an obligation to establish some form of apprentice training for the untrained members of the staff.

Standards in Training

One fundamental consideration which must be borne in mind in considering the training of social case workers is that social case work is one form of social work. Social work itself tends towards the same unity that we have recognized within the general field of social case work. Generic social work is as valid and important a conception as generic social case work. Social case workers must be trained as social workers, which means that the foundation of training for generic social case work must be the same in character as the foundation of training for generic social work. The acceptance of this point of view still leaves us with the problem of defining the content of generic social work, which we can probably not do any more precisely than we have been able to define the content of generic social case work. Nevertheless the acceptance of this point of view would imply one standard of training helpful in the matter of breadth and scope if not in the matter of definition of content.

A second step in progress will be made if we can agree that, while various types of training programs are needed, there must be but one educational standard for all of them. This does not mean that all training programs must be advanced rather than elementary, graduate rather than undergraduate, or equal from the point of view of time required. It means that within the limits of the purposes defined for any training program its training methods and procedures must be educationally consistent with the highest standard that it is possible to formulate. So far as we are aware, no formal training, either in a school or in an apprentice agency, now covers more than two years. It is possible to offer training which will contribute substantially to the professional equipment of social case workers in less than two years. Better training can be given in a longer period. We, therefore, recognize a distinct place, in view of the present demand for social case workers, for training activities that are restricted in the point of time. In setting up a training program to meet a definite need in a local situation or to meet current conditions in any one field of social case work, these two considerations should be borne in mind:

1. There is a minimum educational standard involved both in the element of time and in the quality of instruction, below which a training scheme may cease to have value and may be a positive menace.
2. Every training program should be so organized as to tend towards development in the direction of the best training which has yet been established either in a school or in an apprentice scheme.

In other words, while the scope of a training program may be determined by local or transitory considerations, its character and standards must be determined by the best that there is anywhere in the country.

We have recognized the necessity for apprentice training under present conditions. Moreover we believe that, wisely administered and studied, apprentice training can make a distinct contribution to the development of standards of professional education. In terms of present need, apprentice training in many places is justifying itself in terms of its output. We should like to suggest, however, the following additional arguments for its further development:

1. The schools for some time to come will be unable to turn out sufficient graduates to meet the demand for workers in the field.
2. Nowhere do the present programs of professional education show greater need than for the development of high, stable, educational standards in planned and supervised experience. Practically all planned and super-

vised experience as a part of professional education must be provided through agencies for social case work. In the long run, therefore, the development of practice in social case work as a part of professional education depends upon the educational standards maintained by social case work agencies. We believe that progress towards the solution of this problem will be facilitated through the maintenance for the time being of both apprentice training and schools of social work, each main taining high educational standards.

3. The subject matter of professional education for social case work represents formulations from the practice of social case work on the one hand and from theoretical social science on the other. Without social case work agencies responsibly interested in the training of students, the development of professional education may be unduly influenced by theoretical social science, and the reverse is also true. Apprentice training for the time being provides an opportunity to incorporate into the body of knowledge available for the purposes of professional education whatever of educational value there is in the experience of social case workers and to insure that this analysis and interpretation of experience is carried on unhampered by academic restrictions.

We make our recommendations for the development of apprentice training without reservations. Nevertheless, we believe that the only sound ultimate development must be the organization of professional education in schools of social work. Such schools must always be allied with agencies for social case work in order to provide the field training which we believe to be indispensable. We look forward, therefore, to a system of professional education under the leadership of schools of social work but in alliance with agencies for social case work, the two having co-operative responsibility for one program for professional education and sharing the same educational objectives and standards.

The inherent advantages of the school program over the apprentice program as an ultimate development to be promoted as rapidly as possible may be stated as follows:

1. The professional school comes nearer than apprentice agencies to insuring a full two years of training for the new worker.

2. The school, by reason of its detachment from other administrative responsibility can more nearly insure a distinctly educational approach to the training of the student and therefore runs less risk of exploiting the student for the administrative requirements of the agency.

3. The faculty of the school offers a range and average of ability for educational purposes greater than that of an agency staff which is recruited primarily for other purposes.

4. The possible self-interest of an agency in the evaluation of the planned experiences of the students is likely, under a school training, to be checked when necessary by its sharing of the educational responsibility with the faculty of the school.

5. The training resources of the apprentice agency are naturally limited to its own facilities. The training resources of the school are not so limited and the school may, therefore, provide a greater diversity within the desirable unity of the training scheme.

6. The school may be more successful in getting the students into the spirit of study and in the development of a professional atmosphere than is possible in an agency.

7. The school may have a greater choice of field work for its students among specific fields than is open to any one agency.

8. Students taking the full two-year course in the school are two years older and therefore more mature before they embark upon the complete responsibilities which are expected even of students in an apprentice scheme.

9. The school is more susceptible to social control as an educational institution than an apprentice plan which has a training program not correlated with other educational programs.

10. The school ordinarily has better records of students than an apprentice agency can be expected to keep.

11. The school ordinarily can achieve a better balance among the varied teaching methods and training experiences discussed in this report than is possible for the apprentice agency.

The Stake of the Field in Professional Education

The present contacts of agencies for social case work with the training of social case workers are as follows:

The programs of apprentice training.

The provision of field work in schools of social work.

The release of staff members for part-time teaching in schools.

The maintenance of scholarships for staff members and prospective staff members for work in training schools.

The use of extension and institute courses for the development of staff members.

Although training for social case workers has developed rapidly, and interest in it even more rapidly, the present situation presents great problems as we indicated at the beginning of this section. Our discussions in this section, we believe, point towards progress in solving these problems. Substantial progress in solving these problems requires a greater degree of coherence among agencies and individuals interested in training than now exists. The schools maintain a somewhat loose association for the discussion of their common problems but social case work agencies have little opportunity to participate in their deliberations. Some of the national social case work agencies have committees on training and the Milford Conference has concerned itself with the problem.

Nevertheless there is not any such formally constituted group with continuing responsibility for leadership in this matter representing the field of social case work as is represented by the Standing Committee of the American Academy of Medicine on medical education. We suggest, therefore, that steps should be taken under the wing of some recognized profession-wide organization, to establish a permanent commission or council on education for social work. We believe that both apprentice training and training in the schools would be strengthened at the present time if there were some center through which those responsible for administering professional education could receive from the field authoritative and well-developed suggestions as to what the term "trained social worker" really implies. Looking to the future, we believe that, in the development of professional education for social case work in training schools which are adequate to meet the needs of the agencies, the leadership of the field itself in co-operation with the leadership of the schools is indispensable.